history at source

THE USSR *1945-1990*

John Laver

Hodder & Stoughton
LONDON   ORONTO

ACKNOWLEDGEMENTS

The cover illustration 'We have "reformed" ' is by Nikolai Usov (1987). One of the meanings of the word *perestroika* is military. Here the bureaucratic opponents of *perestroika* have re-grouped under the banner of protocol and contractual clauses (§). Their shields read: 'Red tape', 'Bribe-taking', 'Careerism', 'Incompetence', 'Bureaucratism', 'Show' and 'Conformism'.

The Publishers would like to thank the following for permission to reproduce material in this volume:
   Marion Boyars Publishers Ltd for the poem 'The Statues Sundered Plinth' by Alexander Tvardovsky from *The Russian Poets 1953–68*; Novosti Publishers (APN) for the extract from *What's Good for the Farmer is Good for the Country* by V. Nikonov (1989) and the extract from *The Roots of European Security* by V. Nekrasov (1984).
   The Publishers would also like to acknowledge the following for use of their material: Bantam Books for the extract from *Krushchev Remembers* by N. S. Krushchev (1971); Alfred A. Knopf for the extract from *Progress, Co-existence and Intellectual Freedom* by A. Sakharov (1947) and the extract from *On Socialist Democracy* by R. Medvedev (1975); Macmillan Publishers Ltd for the extract 'Encounters with Krushchev' from *Krushchev and Krushchevism* (1987) ed. M. McCauley; Progress Publishers for the extract from *A Dictionary of Scientific Communism* (English Edition 1984) and the extract from *History of the USSR* by Y. Kukushkin (1984); Public Affairs Press for the extract from *The Economy of the USSR during World War II* by N. A. Voznesensky (1948).
   Every effort has been made to trace and acknowledge ownership of copyright. The publishers will be glad to make suitable arrangements with any copyright holders whom it has not been possible to contact.

BRITISH LIBRARY CATALOGUING-IN-PUBLICATION DATA
Laver, John
   The USSR 1945–90. – (History at source)
   I. Title II. Series
   947.085

   ISBN 0–340–54917–3

First published 1991

© 1991 John Laver

Phototypeset by Intype, London
Printed in Great Britain for the educational publishing division of Hodder and Stoughton Ltd., Mill Road, Dunton Green, Sevenoaks, Kent by Page Brothers Ltd, Norwich

CONTENTS

PREFACE

In recent years there has been an increasing interest in modern Soviet history, partly as the result of rapid developments in the USSR in the Gorbachev era. There has long been a considerable body of literature on Soviet history, and it is a popular topic with students studying at A Level, AS Level, Higher Grade and beyond. It is also true that changes in the requirements of examination boards, particularly the introduction of source-based questions, coursework and personal assignments, have increased the demands on students and teachers alike.

This book is intended for students, and hopefully teachers, who are interested in a number of key topics in Soviet history and would benefit from a practical complement to existing textbooks and monographs. A number of central issues and topics are introduced through collections of primary and secondary sources, together with questions of the type likely to be encountered in examinations or other exercises involving use of sources. Practical advice is proffered on the way to approach such questions, and a specimen is included. Guidance is also offered on the approach to essay questions. Sample essay titles are given along with suggestions on relevant approaches; and again, a specimen answer is included. Finally, an analytical bibliography is intended to give guidance to teachers and students alike.

It is hoped that this collection will prove useful for students working as part of an organised course or on their own.

APPROACHING SOURCE-BASED QUESTIONS

Source-based questions have become an important part of History examinations at all levels in recent years. Students who have studied History at GCSE and Standard Grade level will be used to handling various types of sources. The skills they have learned in handling evidence will continue to be applicable at a more advanced level, but there will also be more sophisticated skills to master and the sources themselves may be more demanding.

During your studies you will encounter both primary and secondary historical evidence. The distinction between the two is sometimes artificially exaggerated: all sources have their value and limitations, and it is possible to worry unnecessarily about a 'hierarchy of sources'. The important thing for the student is to feel confident in handling all sources. The majority of sources in this book are primary sources, since they are the raw material from which historians work. Many are of a documentary nature, since that is the type most commonly found in examinations. However, there are also statistics and many examples of visual evidence. The comments below will usually apply to *all* types of evidence.

When a student is faced with a piece of historical evidence, there are certain questions that he or she should always ask of that source; but in an examination that student will be asked specific questions set by an examiner and, in the light of pressures, not least of which is time, it is important to approach these questions in an organised and coherent fashion.

The following advice should be borne in mind when answering source-based questions. Some of the advice may appear obvious in the cold light of day, but, as examiners will testify, the obvious is often ignored in the cauldron of the examination room!

1 Read the sources carefully before attempting to answer the questions, whether there is one source or a collection of them. This will give you an overview of the sources which will usually be connected and related to a particular theme. You will study the individual sources in detail when you answer specific questions.

2 Always look carefully at the attribution of the sources: the author and date of publication; the recipient, if any; the context in which the source was produced. All these will often give you an insight in addition to that provided by the content of the source itself.

3 Mark allocations are usually given at the end of each question or sub-question. Ignore the marks at your peril! The number of marks will almost certainly give you some indication of the length of answer expected. Length of answer is not an indicator of quality, and there is no such thing as a standard answer, but it is commonplace for candidates in examinations to write paragraph-length answers to questions carrying one or two marks. A question carrying such a low mark can usually be adequately answered in two or three sentences. You do not have the time to waste your purple prose in examinations! Similarly, a mark allocation of nine or ten marks indicates the expectation of a reasonably substantial answer.

4 Study the wording of the questions very carefully. Some questions will ask you to use *only* your own knowledge in the answer; some will ask you to use *both* your own knowledge *and* the source(s); some will insist that you confine your answer to knowledge gleaned from the

source(s) *alone*. If you ignore the instructions, you will certainly deprive yourself of marks.

5 If there are several sources to be consulted, ensure that you make use of the ones to which you are directed – candidates have been known to ignore some or choose the wrong ones.

6 Certain types of question require a particular type of response:
   a) Comparison and/or contrasting of sources: ensure that you do consider all the sources referred to in the question.
   b) Testing the usefulness and limitations of sources: if you are asked to do both, ensure that you do consider both aspects. You may be required to evaluate a source in relation to other information provided, or in the context of your own background knowledge of the subject.
   c) Testing reliability: this is not the same as considering the utility of a source, although students sometimes confuse the two concepts.
   d) Phrases such as 'Comment upon', 'Analyse' or 'Assess': ensure that you do what is asked. Do not be afraid of quoting extracts from a source in your answer, but avoid over-quotation or too much direct paraphrasing, since questions will usually, although not always, be testing more than comprehension, and therefore you should simply be illustrating or amplifying a particular point. Always *use* the sources and do not just regurgitate what is in front of you.
   e) Synthesis: this is a high level skill which requires you to blend several pieces of evidence and draw general conclusions.

7 If at all possible, avoid spending too much time on the sources questions in examinations. Frequently candidates answer the sources questions thoroughly but do not allow themselves enough time to do justice to the rest of the examination paper, and essay answers sometimes suffer in consequence if they are attempted last.

8 If possible, read published examiners' reports which will give you further indication as to the most useful approaches to particular questions, and the pitfalls to avoid.

A Note on this Collection of Sources

It is the intention of this collection to give ideas to teachers and realistic examples of sources and questions to students, either for use in schools and colleges or for self-study purposes. However, they are intended to be flexible. If it is found helpful, adapt the questions or mark allocations; or devise new questions; or use the sources as part of coursework or personal studies. You might even find it an interesting exercise to put together your own sources and appropriate questions.

1 STALIN SUPREME 1945–53

The USSR narrowly survived the German invasion of 1941, but then, after a long and costly struggle, emerged from the Second World War as one of the World's two Superpowers, together with the USA. The USSR became arbiter not just of its own fate, but of that of many other countries. Many Soviet citizens hoped that victory in the War and the experience of closer relations with Western democracies would lead to a relaxation of political and social controls within their own country. Such optimism was quickly quashed, as Stalinism in all its extreme pre-War manifestations was reimposed; indeed the process had begun before the War was over.

After 1945 Stalin did not exercise such close personal control over day to day affairs. Nevertheless, most Russians would not have noticed the difference. Real or imagined traitors were imprisoned or worse; a campaign against foreign influences, or 'cosmopolitanism', was launched; and the Party reasserted control over the Army and other institutions.

Domestically, the greatest achievement of the Soviets in the post-War period was to recover, at least in some spheres, from the devastation of the War itself. Industrial recovery seems to have been quite rapid, and the real income of workers began to rise. However, social improvements scarcely kept pace: existing deficiencies in housing and social services had been exacerbated by the War; freedom in religion and cultural life was completely stifled. Stalin and Stalinism reigned supreme.

Assessments of Stalin since his death have been notable for the strength of reaction displayed. Controversy has centred on such issues as: was Stalin a Marxist or did he betray socialist principles? Did he simply extend and refine brutal tendencies inherent in the USSR since the Revolution? Could Stalin have transformed Russia into a Superpower and won the War without imposing a totalitarian political system? Particularly during the Gorbachev era, Stalin has received much posthumous criticism. However, many Russians of the old Stalinist generation still look back nostalgically to the days of the 'Red Tsar', and surveys of younger Russians indicate a sizeable minority that yearns for a return to the strong leadership associated with Stalin's name.

A Post-War Optimism

I firmly believed that after victory everything would suddenly change. . . . When I recall conversations at the front and at the rear, when I re-read letters, it is clear that everybody expected that once victory had been won, people would know real happiness. We realised, of course, that the country had been devastated, impoverished, that we would have to work hard, and we did not have fantasies about mountains of gold. But we believed that victory would bring justice, that human dignity would triumph.

Ilya Ehrenburg: *The War 1941–45* (1964)

B The Impact of War

The material damage inflicted on the economy of the USSR by Hitlerite Germany and her accomplices can be expressed in terms of the loss of output and income by the population and the state as a result of the cessation of production in the occupied territory of the USSR. . . .

The following failed to be produced, and consequently were lost to the economy, in the occupied regions and enterprises of the USSR during the period of the Patriotic War only: 307 million tons of hard coal, 72 billion kilowatt-hours of electric power, 38 million tons of steel, 136 thousand tons of aluminium, 58 thousand tractors, 90 thousand metal-cutting machine tools, 68 million quintals of sugar, 11 billion poods of grain, 1,922 million quintals of potatoes, 68 million quintals of meat, and 567 million quintals of milk. . . .

The Soviet people is reconstructing the national economy of the USSR with its heroic efforts, and will surpass the prewar level of production and overtake economically the main capitalist countries. The peoples of the USSR, manifesting an extraordinary will to work and straining their spiritual and physical powers, will successfully solve these historic problems.

The material loss inflicted by Hitlerite Germany on the peoples of the Soviet Union is being to a negligible extent compensated by the relocation of industrial equipment from Germany to the USSR in the form of reparations. The value of this equipment amounts to only 0.6 per cent of the magnitude of just the 'direct property losses' borne by the USSR during the Patriotic War. . . . The restoration of production in the liberated regions of the USSR, and the liquidation of the effects of German occupation, are proceeding on the basis of socialist production, which had demonstrated during the Patriotic War its stability and its great superiority over the capitalist economy.

N. A. Voznesensky: *The Economy Of The USSR During World War II* (1948)

C Stalin Faces The Future

The Communist Party's plans of work for the immediate future . . .
are set forth in the new Five-Year Plan which is shortly to be endorsed.
The principal aims of the new Five-Year Plan are to rehabilitate the
ravaged areas of the country, to restore the pre-war level in industry
and agriculture, and then to surpass this level in more or less
substantial measure. To say nothing of the fact that the rationing
system will shortly be abolished (*stormy, prolonged applause*).
Special attention will be devoted to extending the production of
consumer goods, to raising the living standard of the working people
by steadily lowering the prices of all goods (*stormy, prolonged
applause*). . . .

With regard to the plans for a longer period ahead, the Party means
to organise a new mighty upsurge in the national economy, which
would allow us to increase our industrial production, for example,
three times over as compared with the pre-war period. . . . Only under
such conditions can we consider that our homeland will be
guaranteed against all possible accidents (*stormy applause*). That
will take three more Five-Year Plans, I should think, if not more. But
it can be done and we must do it (*stormy applause*). . . .

The Communist Party is prepared to accept the electors' verdict
(*stormy applause*).

In the election struggle the Communist Party is not alone. It goes
to the polls in a bloc with non-Party people. In bygone days the
Communists treated non-Party people and non-Party status with some
mistrust. . . . But now we have different times. Our non-Party people
are now divided from the bourgeoisie by a barrier known as the Soviet
social order. This same barrier unites non-Party people with the
Communists in a single community of Soviet men and women. . . .
The important thing is that both are furthering the same common
cause. Therefore the bloc of Communists and non-Party people is a
natural and vital thing (*stormy, prolonged applause*). . . .

(*All rise. Prolonged, unabating applause turning into an ovation.
From all parts of the hall come cheers: 'Long live our great Stalin!
Hurrah!' 'Hurrah for the great leader of the peoples!' 'Glory to the
great Stalin!' 'Long live Comrade Stalin, the candidate of the entire
nation!' 'Glory to Comrade Stalin, the creator of all our victories!'.*)

Stalin's pre-election speech, 9 February 1946

D The Post-War Economy
THE FOURTH FIVE-YEAR PLAN

	1940	1945	1950 (Plan)	1950 (Actual)
National Income (index)	100	83	138	164
Gross Industrial Production	100	92	148	173
Producers' Goods	100	112	–	205
Consumers' Goods	100	59	–	123
Gross Agricultural Production	100	60	127	99
Coal (million tons)	165.9	149.3	250	261.1
Electricity (milliard kwhs)	48.3	43.2	82	91.2
Oil (million tons)	31.1	19.4	35.4	37.9
Steel (million tons)	18.3	12.3	25.4	27.3
Cement (million tons)	5.7	1.8	10.5	10.2
Sugar (million tons)	2.2	0.46	2.4	2.5
Leather Footwear (million pairs)	211	63	240	203.4
Tractors (thousands)	66.2	14.7	112	242.5
Workers and Employees (millions)	31.2	27.3	33.5	39.2

From Soviet sources

E Propaganda For The Masses

(i) 'Fulfil the Five-Year Plan in four years!' 1948 Poster.

4

(ii) 'Work hard during harvest time and you'll be rewarded with plenty of bread.' 1947 Poster.

F An 'Official' View Of Stalin

Stalin is the brilliant leader and teacher of the Party, the great strategist of the Socialist Revolution, military commander, and guide of the Soviet state. An implacable attitude towards the enemies of Socialism; profound fidelity to principle; a combination of clear revolutionary perspective and clarity of purpose with extraordinary firmness and persistence in the pursuit of aims; wise and practical leadership; and intimate contact with the masses – such are the characteristic features of Stalin's style. . . .

Stalin guides the destinies of a multi-national Socialist state, a state of workers and peasants, of which there is no precedent in history. . . . The range of questions which engage his attention is immense, embracing complex problems of Marxist-Leninist theory and school textbooks; problems of Soviet foreign policy and the municipal affairs of Moscow, the proletarian capital . . . the advancement of Soviet literature and art and the editing of the model rules for collective farms; and lastly, the solution of most intricate theoretical and practical problems in the science of warfare. . . .

Everybody is familiar with the cogent and invincible force of Stalin's logic, the crystal clarity of his mind, his iron will, his devotion to the Party, his ardent faith in the people, and love for the people. Everybody is familiar with his modesty, his simplicity of manner, his consideration for people, and his merciless severity towards enemies of the people. Everybody is familiar with his intolerance of ostentation, of phrasemongers and windbags, of whiners and alarmists. Stalin is wise and deliberate in solving complex political questions where a thorough weighing of advantages and disadvantages is required. At the same time, he is a supreme master of bold revolutionary decisions and of swift adaptations to changed conditions.

Stalin is the worthy continuer of the cause of Lenin, or, as it is said in the Party: Stalin is the Lenin of today.

G. Alexandrov: *Joseph Stalin: A Short Biography* (Moscow 1947)

G Malenkov's Report To The Party

. . . It would be a mistake not to see that the level of Party political work still lags behind the demands of life, the tasks put forward by the Party. It must be admitted that there are defects and errors in the work of the Party organisations and that there are still many negative, and at times even unhealthy, phenomena in the life of our Party organisations. . . .

The role of criticism and self-criticism in the life of the Party and state is still underestimated in the Party organisations; persecution and victimisation for criticism occur. One can still meet officials who never stop shouting about their devotion to the Party but actually tolerate no criticism from below, stifle it and take revenge on those who criticise them. . . .

The Party does not need hardened and indifferent bureaucrats who prefer their own peace of mind to the interests of work, but tireless and selfless fighters for fulfilment of the directives of the Party and government who place the interests of the state above all else. . . .

Ideological work is a paramount duty of the Party and underestimation of it may do irreparable damage to the interests of the Party and the state. We must always remember that any weakening of the influence of the socialist ideology signifies a strengthening of the influence of bourgeois ideology. . . .

Comrade Stalin's writings are a vivid indication of the outstanding importance our Party attaches to theory. . . . Comrade Stalin's discoveries in the field of theory have world-historical importance and arm all peoples with knowledge of the ways of revolutionary transformation of society and with our Party's wealth of experience in the struggle for communism.

The immense significance of Comrade Stalin's works of theory is that they warn us against skimming the surface; they penetrate the heart of phenomena, the very essence of society's development; they teach us to perceive in embryo the factors which will determine the course of events, which make possible Marxist prognosis.

Malenkov's report to the Nineteenth Party Congress, October 1952

Questions

1 Using your own knowledge, explain the grounds for optimism of Russians such as Ehrenburg at the end of the Second World War.

(3 marks)

2 What do Sources B and D suggest about the damage inflicted on the USSR by the Second World War? **(6 marks)**

3 a) What does Source D suggest were the priorities of the Soviet economy after 1945? **(4 marks)**

b) To what extent does Source D suggest that the targets of the Fourth Five-Year Plan were fulfilled? **(5 marks)**

c) Does Source D suggest that the expectations of Sources B and C were fulfilled? **(6 marks)**

4 What does Source C suggest were Stalin's priorities after 1945?

(4 marks)

5 a) Identify and compare the elements of propaganda in Sources C, E and F. **(7 marks)**

  b) Using your own knowledge, explain the circumstances in which any two of these pieces of propaganda were produced. **(4 marks)**

6 To what extent do Sources A–F suggest that Stalinism after the Second World War retained its earlier characteristics? **(10 marks)**

2 THE USSR AND THE COLD WAR
1945–53

At the end of the Second World War the USSR had authority over much of Eastern and South-Eastern Europe. Many Western politicians maintained their inherent suspicion of what they perceived as the expansionist tendencies of Communism. However, there was also a general perception that world peace could be maintained only if the USSR, as a Superpower, played a prominent role in international affairs. Indeed, the Soviets helped to establish the United Nations Organisation and took part in some important conferences, such as Potsdam.

The menace of Nazi Germany was gone, and with it the cement of the wartime alliance. A series of events initiated a period of hostility between the USSR and the West which became known as the Cold War: the establishment of Soviet control over Eastern Europe; the Marshall Plan and the Truman Doctrine; the setting up of the Cominform; disputes over Germany which culminated in the Berlin Blockade, the division of the country and the creation of NATO; the Soviet acquisition of the atom bomb; and the Korean War.

Interpretations of the Cold War during the Stalin era have undergone several shifts. By the late 1940s the 'orthodox' Western interpretation was that the Cold War was the product of the Marxist-Leninist doctrine of class warfare and world revolution: the USSR was intent on undermining the Free World and paving the way for world Communism, a threat which had to be countered by a firm Western stand including military alliances and measures to promote political and economic cooperation.

A later 'revisionist' interpretation exonerated Stalin for much of the blame for the Cold War. Instead it was argued that the USSR, emerging from a costly War in 1945, faced the threat of a powerful USA with a nuclear monopoly. World revolution was not on Stalin's agenda: rather a concern to effect economic recovery and establish a buffer zone of security in Eastern Europe. The events outlined above could be interpreted as legitimate attempts by the USSR to counter American economic and political imperialism.

Both of these interpretations appear somewhat simplistic. Both the USA and USSR had been essentially isolationist in their foreign policies before the War, had little knowledge of each other, and were bound to experience difficulties in the post-War manoeuvrings as a new Europe emerged. It is dangerous to assume that Stalin had a coherent long-term strategy other than to protect and extend Russia's security.

9

It was in his nature to react to events. Unfortunately when he did react, as in the case of Berlin, the reaction was sometimes clumsy. However, many of his promises were kept. His interpretation of Yalta may have been different from many Americans, but he did reduce the size of the Red Army by 1948, he had no plans to invade surrounding states such as Greece or Turkey, and most of the disagreements arose from attempts to establish precisely where the boundaries lay between Western and Soviet spheres of influence. Stalin did not manipulate the world Communist movement in the simplistic manner often portrayed, and he never lost his natural caution in foreign affairs any more than in those of a domestic nature.

A Stalin's Reply To Churchill's 'Iron Curtain' Speech

... Mr. Churchill now takes the stand of the warmongers, and in this Mr. Churchill is not alone. He has friends not only in Britain but in the United States of America as well.

A point to be noted is that in this respect Mr. Churchill and his friends bear a striking resemblance to Hitler and his friends. . . . Mr. Churchill sets out to unleash war with a race theory, asserting that only English-speaking nations are superior nations, who are called upon to decide the destinies of the entire world. . . .

The following circumstances should not be forgotten. The Germans made their invasion of the USSR through Finland, Poland, Rumania, Bulgaria and Hungary. The Germans were able to make their invasion through these countries because at the time, governments hostile to the Soviet Union existed in these countries. As a result of the German invasion, in the fighting and through the deportation of Soviet citizens to German servitude, the Soviet Union has lost a total of about seven million people. In other words, the Soviet Union's loss of life has been several times greater than that of Britain and the United States of America put together. Possibly in some quarters an inclination is felt to forget about these colossal sacrifices of the Soviet people which secured the liberation of Europe from the Hitlerite yoke. But the Soviet Union cannot forget about them. And so what is surprising about the fact that the Soviet Union, anxious for its future safety, is trying to ensure that governments loyal in their attitude to the Soviet Union should exist in these countries? How can anyone, who has not taken leave of his senses, describe these peaceful aspirations of the Soviet Union as expansionist tendencies on the part of our state?

Interview with Stalin printed in *Pravda*, 13 March 1946

B Molotov's Apprehension About American Economic Power

We know that the United States made a very great effort in this war, in defence of its own interets and of our common aims, for which we are all very grateful to the United States. But for all that, it cannot be said that the United States is one of those states which suffered grave material damage in the Second World War, which were ruined and weakened in this war. . . .

It is surely not so difficult to understand that if American capital were given a free hand in the small states ruined and enfeebled by the war, as the advocates of the principles of 'equal opportunity' desire, American capital would buy up the local industries, appropriate the more attractive Rumanian, Yugoslav and other enterprises, and would become the master in these small states. . . . Is it not clear that such unrestricted application of the principle of 'equal opportunity' in the given conditions would in practice mean the veritable economic enslavement of the small states and their subjugation to the rule and arbitrary will of strong and enriched foreign firms, banks and industrial companies . . . Was this what we fought for when we battled the Fascist invaders, the Hitlerite and Japanese imperialists?

Speech by Soviet Foreign Minister Molotov, 10 October 1946

C More Soviet Apprehension

President Truman has announced the following principles of American foreign policy: the United States will support with weapons and money reactionaries and Fascists everywhere who are hateful to their own people but who are ready to place their country under American control. Two countries suitable for this were found at once: Greece and Turkey. Both have come under American domination. Americans are building their military bases there. American capitalists are opening businesses and buying up all that seems to them profitable. For this the Greek and Turkish reactionaries, who are in power, are receiving from the Americans money and weapons for the struggle against their own people. But Greece and Turkey are too small, and American expansionists are dreaming of all Europe, or at least Western Europe. Directly to propose that the European countries become American colonies such as Greece and Turkey is somewhat inconvenient. And so the 'Marshall Plan' emerges in America. It was announced that the United States wanted to 'help' the European countries to reconstruct their war-destroyed economies. Many believed this. But it was soon evident that the 'Marshall Plan' was simply a cunning way of subjecting all Europe to American capital.

Article in young peoples' newspaper *Pionerskaya Pravda*, August 1947

D Soviet Complaints About American Policy

The so-called Truman Doctrine and the Marshall Plan are particularly glaring examples of the manner in which the principles of the United

Nations are violated, and of the way in which the Organisation is ignored.

As the experience of the past few months has shown, the proclamation of this doctrine has meant that the United States Government has moved toward a direct renunciation of the principles of international collaboration and concerted action by the great Powers and toward attempts to impose its will on other independent states. At the same time the United States is using the economic resources distributed as relief to individual needy nations as an instrument of political pressure. . . .

As is now clear, the Marshall Plan constitutes in essence merely a variant of the Truman Doctrine adapted to the conditions of post-war Europe. . . . It is becoming more and more evident to everyone that the implementation of the Marshall Plan will mean placing European countries under the economic and political control of the United States and direct interference by the latter in the internal affairs of those countries.

Moreover, this Plan is an attempt to split Europe into two camps and, with the help of the United Kingdom and France, to complete the formation of a *bloc* of several European countries hostile to the interests of the democratic countries of Eastern Europe and most particularly to the interests of the Soviet Union.

Speech by Soviet Foreign Minister Vyshinsky at the United Nations, 18 September 1947

Questions

1 Using your own knowledge, explain the significance of Churchill's 'Iron Curtain' speech to which Stalin was replying in Source A.

(5 marks)

2 Identify Stalin's main concerns in foreign policy as revealed in Source A. **(6 marks)**

3 Compare Sources B, C and D in their assessment of Soviet objections to American foreign policy in the years to 1947. **(8 marks)**

4 Take any one of Sources A–D and assess its uses and limitations to an historian investigating the origins of the Cold War. **(5 marks)**

5 Using Sources A–D, and your own knowledge, examine the extent to which the Cold War was firmly established by 1947. **(10 marks)**

3 Krushchev's Russia

Following Stalin's death in 1953 there was considerable manoeuvring for power by leading Party figures. The foremost contender appeared to be Malenkov, but he was effectively challenged by colleagues. Krushchev himself did not emerge as *the* clear successor until 1957: backed by the Army and industrial pressure-groups, he promptly adopted Malenkov's platform of promoting living standards ('Goulash Communism') and advocating agricultural reform.

Krushchev had to devote considerable energy to defeating opponents within the Praesidium. When ousted, these opponents, labelled the 'Anti-Party Group', suffered demotion or disgrace, a change from the harsher measures taken during Stalin's office.

Krushchev effectively shaped Soviet domestic and foreign policy until 1964. However, some entrenched opposition remained to limit the impact of certain attempted reforms; for example, efforts to broaden the social basis of higher education.

Krushchev's expertise was in agriculture. Between 1954 and 1958 agricultural output was greatly increased, as peasants and workers in state farms were given more benefits and incentives. However, production then faltered again and the much-publicised Virgin Lands scheme failed.

In other areas of the economy, a policy of decentralisation was adopted, chiefly through the creation of regional economic councils. However, the ambitious Five and Seven Year Plans did not fulfil expectations and reform was sometimes sabotaged by reluctant officials afraid of losing the security of their positions. Some social advances were initiated, but the USSR failed to match and overtake the West in prosperity as Krushchev had optimistically boasted.

In both his foreign and domestic policies Krushchev faced opposition and discontent. This opposition developed at most levels of the Party, since proposed reforms threatened privilege and security of tenure; it also occurred within the ranks of erstwhile supporters, most notably the Army. Dislike of Krushchev's unpredictability and personality cult fuelled opposition, and he was forced out of office in 1964. Although Krushchev had attempted to alter the Stalinist structure of Russia, he lacked the determination or widespread support necessary to effect any substantial and long-term changes.

A Krushchev Triumphant

At its meetings of 22 June to 29 June 1957, the plenary session of the Party Central Committee considered the question of the anti-Party group of Malenkov, Kaganovitch and Molotov, which had formed within the Praesidium of the Party Central Committee. . . .

Seeking to change the Party's political line, this group used anti-Party, factional methods in an attempt to change the composition of the Party's leading bodies, elected by the plenary session of the Party Central Committee. . . .

This group persistently opposed and sought to frustrate the reorganisation of industrial management and the setting up of economic councils in the economic regions, a vastly important measure approved by the entire Party and the people. . . .

With regard to agricultural questions, the members of this group failed to understand the new and vital tasks. They did not acknowledge the need to increase material incentives for the collective farm peasantry in increasing the output of agricultural products. They opposed abolition of the old bureaucratic system of planning on the collective farms and the introduction of the new system of planning which unleashes the initiative of the collective farms in managing their own affairs. . . .

Comrades Malenkov, Kaganovitch and Molotov stubbornly opposed those measures which the Central Committee and our entire Party carried out to eliminate the consequences of the cult of the individual leader, to eliminate the violations of revolutionary law which had occurred and to create conditions which would preclude their recurrence. . . .

. . . The plenary session of the Party Central Committee resolves: To condemn as incompatible with the Leninist principles of our Party the factional activities of the anti-Party group of Malenkov, Kaganovitch and Molotov, and of Shepilov, who joined them. . . .

Resolution of the Central Committee of the Communist party, 29 June 1957

B Krushchev Promises A Bright Future

In the current decade (1961–70) the Soviet Union, in creating the material and technical basis of communism, will surpass the strongest and richest capitalist country, the USA, in production per head of population; the people's standard of living and their cultural and technical standards will improve substantially; everyone will live in easy circumstances; all collective and state farms will become highly productive and profitable enterprises; the demand of Soviet people for well-appointed housing will, in the main, be satisfied; hard physical work will disappear; the USSR will have the shortest working day.

The material and technical basis of communism will be built up by the *end of the second decade* (1971–80), ensuring an abundance of material and cultural values for the whole population; Soviet society will come close to a stage where it can introduce the principle of distribution according to needs, and there will be a gradual transition to one form of ownership – national ownership. Thus, *a communist society will be built in the USSR.* . . .

All-round extension and perfection of socialist democracy, active participation of all citizens in the administration of the state, in the management of economic and cultural development, improvement of the government apparatus, and increased control over its activity by the people constitute the main direction in which socialist statehood develops in the building of communism. As socialist democracy develops, the organs of state power will gradually be transformed into organs of public self-government. . . .

The Party considers that the paramount task in the ideological field in the present period is to educate all working people in a spirit of ideological integrity and devotion to communism, and cultivate in them a communist attitude to labour and the social economy; to eliminate completely the survivals of bourgeois views and morals. . . .

The period of full-scale communist construction is characterised by a further *enhancement of the role and importance of the Communist Party* as the leading and guiding force of Soviet society. . . .

The Party proceeds from the Marxist-Leninist proposition: history is made by the people, and communism is a creation of the people, of its energy and intelligence. . . .

Programme of the Communist Party of the Soviet Union, adopted by the Twenty-Second Congress, 31 October 1961

C The Fall Of Krushchev

Krushchev allowed serious mistakes in his work, made thoughtless and hasty decisions, and played organisational leap-frog.

In recent years Krushchev concentrated all the power in the country in his own hands and began to abuse it. He attributed all the achievements of the country to his own personal merits, completely ceased to consider the members of the Praesidium, slighted them, insulted them, did not listen to their opinions, constantly lectured them and everyone else. . . .

Krushchev surrounded himself with advisers from among his relatives and journalists whose voice he heeded more than the voice of the members of the Praesidium. . . .

The creation at Krushchev's initiative of two party organisations –

industrial and rural – caused much confusion and represents the creation of two new parties, a workers' party and a peasants' party. . . .

Krushchev so confused the administration of industry by creating committees – the Economic Council of the USSR and the Supreme Economic Council of the USSR – that it appears very difficult to untangle all this. Industry is now doing worse. . . .

Krushchev never allowed one member of the Praesidium to go out to the provinces, declaring: 'it is useless for you to go there, they have to work!'

He sometimes reprimanded a member of the Praesidium for measures that had been carried out, forgetting that he had proposed these same measures in speeches that had been written for him earlier. . . .

Could we have called him to order sooner? . . . It is harder to struggle with a living cult than with a dead one. If Stalin destroyed people physically, Krushchev destroyed them morally. The removal of Krushchev from power is a sign not of the weakness but of the strength of the party, and this should be a lesson.

Report of M. Suslov at the Plenum of the Central Committee of the Communist Party, 1964

D Economic Development In The Krushchev Era
AGRICULTURE

Grain Harvest In Millions Of Tons

1950	81.2	1954	85.6	1958	134.7
1951	78.7	1955	103.7	1959	119.5
1952	92.2	1956	125.0	1960	125.5
1953	82.5	1957	102.6	1965	121.1

INDUSTRY

	1955	1965
Oil (millions of tons)	170.0	507.0
Coal (millions of tons)	390.0	578.0
Iron (millions of tons)	33.3	66.2
Electricity (milliards of Kwh)	170.0	507.0
Tractors (thousands)	163.0	355.0

Statistics principally from Soviet Sources

E A British Ambassador Reminisces
Krushchev often reminded me of the driver of an autocar too big and heavy for his skills, too often pressing his foot down on the accelerator around dangerous bends and too often having jerkily to

apply the brakes. He lacked Stalin's basic caution, so much closer to Russian traditional policies, and embarked confidently upon adventurous courses with attractive options without seeing clearly where they might lead him. When the risks became too great, he had to beat hasty retreats, usually skilfully conducted, but finally trying too far the nerves and patience of his colleagues. Nor did he acquire the confident support of the Soviet population, despite all he had done to free them from Stalin's tyranny. They instinctively felt his behaviour was not that expected of a Russian leader. Worst of all he lost respect by showing himself 'uncultured'. . . . Last but not least, from my point of view as a former Ambassador in Moscow, he was a most accessible, communicative, human and stimulating leader, however adversarial, with whom to do business.

Former British Ambassador in Moscow, F. R. Roberts: 'Encounters With Krushchev' in *Krushchev and Krushchevism* (ed. M. McCauley 1987)

F Russian Jokes About Krushchev
A man ran through the streets of Moscow shouting: 'Krushchev is a swine!'.

He was arrested and given twenty one years: one year for defamation; twenty years for leaking state secrets.

A man was discovered in Moscow who, even when blindfolded, could tell from a skull who it had belonged to.

It was decided to test him. The Authorities blindfolded the man and brought in the skull of Karl Marx. The man felt the skull all over. He declared: 'A theoretician; a thinker.'

Next Lenin's skull was brought in. The man felt it over, and declared: 'A pragmatist with a theoretical streak.'

The authorities were amazed, and led in Krushchev. The man fingered Krushchev's bald head for a few minutes, then declared: 'It's clearly someone's backside, but I can't for the life of me find the hole!'

At the Twentieth Party Congress Krushchev was recounting Stalin's crimes, when a voice came from the back of the hall: 'And where were you then?'

'Would the man who asked that question stand up,' said Krushchev. Nobody stood up.

'That's where we were, too!' replied Krushchev.

Questions

1 What information can be gleaned from Source A about Krushchev's intended reform programme? **(5 marks)**

2 Using your own knowledge, explain the circumstances which led the individuals named in Source A to oppose Krushchev's rise to power. **(6 marks)**

3 What was Krushchev's conception of Communism and the role of the Party as outlined in Source B? **(7 marks)**

4 Does the evidence of Source D:
a) Suggest that the promises made in Source B were implemented? **(5 marks)**
b) Support the criticisms of Krushchev made in Source C? **(5 marks)**

5 Compare and contrast the impression of Krushchev given in Sources E and F. **(6 marks)**

6 What are the uses and limitations of Sources E and F to an historian of Krushchev's Russia? **(8 marks)**

7 Using *only* the evidence of Sources A–F, assess the validity of the statement that in terms of domestic affairs 'The Krushchev period was one of hope and despair'. **(10 marks)**

4 DE-STALINISATION

Krushchev's long political apprenticeship had taken place under Stalin, and in essence he was a committed Stalinist. However, he was also more familiar with popular opinion than some of his colleagues, and he was prepared to take risks, either to improve conditions within the USSR, or, as his detractors claimed, with the aim of asserting his own authority as Stalin's successor.

Whatever Krushchev's real motives, his speech to the Twentieth Congress of the Communist Party in 1956 was remarkable in its denunciation of Stalin for his personality cult and methods of rule; also for its call for a policy of coexistence, rather than confrontation, with the West. Significantly, Krushchev did not attack the essence of the Stalinist system – of which, after all, he was a part – and therefore the Party itself escaped his censure. Nevertheless he was preparing for a further development of the Soviet social and economic system.

Within the USSR de-Stalinisation meant several things: the rehabilitation of certain Stalinist victims; more freedom for writers and artists; more opportunity for debate; a requirement that Party and state organs operate within the law; and moves to promote Krushchev's own supporters to the highest ranks within the Party.

It is probable that the consequences of de-Stalinisation were not foreseen by Krushchev. Particularly alarming was the anti-Soviet reaction in the satellite states – notably Hungary and Poland – and the severance of relations with Mao's China. Strong criticism of Krushchev's policy by his opponents restricted his freedom of action. Orthodox Stalinists were particularly outraged by the apparent freedom to criticise the Soviet system granted to intellectuals such as Solzhenitsyn.

Critics have maintained that Krushchev was only concerned with greater efficiency and improvements in the material standard of living of the Soviet people; they assert that genuine intellectual freedom and liberal values in the Western sense were never his intentions. If so, Krushchev was guilty of opening a dangerous can of worms, and the policy of de-Stalinisation was an important factor in his downfall. Perhaps of greater significance was the question: could the USSR be altered only by tinkering with aspects of the Stalinist system, a system which had been brutally imposed and refined during the previous 25 years? Later reformers decided that a more fundamental restructuring was called for.

A Krushchev Denounces Stalin

Stalin acted not through persuasion, explanation and patient cooperation with people, but by imposing his concepts and demanding absolute submission to his opinion. Whoever opposed this concept, or tried to prove his viewpoint and the correctness of his position, was doomed to removal from the leading collective and to subsequent moral and physical annihilation. . . .

We must affirm that the Party had fought a serious fight against the Trotskyites, rightists and bourgeois nationalists, and that it ideologically disarmed all the enemies of Leninism. This ideological fight was carried on successfully, as a result of which the Party became strengthened and tempered. Here Stalin played a positive role. . . . But some years later, when socialism in our country was fundamentally constructed, when the exploiting classes were generally liquidated, when the Soviet social structure had radically changed, when the social basis for political movements and groups hostile to the Party had violently contracted, when the ideological opponents of the Party were long since defeated politically – then the repression directed against them began.

It was precisely during this period (1935–1938) that the practice of mass repression through the government apparatus was born, first against the enemies of Leninism – Trotskyites, Zinovievites and Bukharinites, long since politically defeated by the Party – and subsequently also against many honest Communists, those Party cadres who had borne the heavy load of the Civil War, and the first and most difficult years of industrialisation and collectivisation, and who had actively fought against the Trotskyites and the rightists for the Leninist Party line.

Stalin originated the concept 'enemy of the people'. . . . This term made possible the usage of the most cruel repression. . . . Facts prove that many abuses were made on Stalin's orders without consulting norms of Party and Soviet legality. Stalin was a very distrustful man, sickly suspicious; we knew this from our work with him. . . . The sickly suspicion created in him a general distrust even towards eminent Party workers whom he had known for years. Everywhere and in everything he saw 'enemies', 'two-facers' and 'spies'. . . .

The wilfulness of Stalin showed itself not only in decisions concerning the internal life of the country, but also in the international relations of the Soviet Union.

The July Plenum of the Central Committee studied in detail the reasons for the development of conflict with Yugoslavia. It was a shameful role which Stalin played here. . . .

Some comrades may ask us: 'Why did members of the Politburo view these matters in different ways at different times'. Initially, many of them backed Stalin actively because he was one of the strongest

Marxists and his logic, his strength and his will greatly influenced the cadres and Party work. . . . And when we consider the fact that in the last years the Central Committee plenary sessions were not convened and that the sessions of the Politburo occurred only occasionally then we will understand how difficult it was for any member of the Politburo to take a stand against one or another unjust or improper procedure, against serious errors and shortcomings in the practices of leadership. . . .

Comrades, we must abolish the cult of the individual decisively . . . and restore completely the Leninist principles of Soviet socialist democracy, expressed in the Constitution of the Soviet Union, to fight the wilfulness of individuals abusing their power. . . . Comrades, the Twentieth Congress of the Communist Party of the Soviet Union has manifested with a new strength the unshakable unity of our Party, its cohesiveness around the Central Committee, its resolute will to accomplish the great task of building Communism. (*Tumultuous applause.*)

We are absolutely certain that our Party, armed with the historical resolutions of the Twentieth Congress, will lead the Soviet people along the Leninist path to new successes, to new victories. (*Tumultuous, prolonged applause.*)

Long live the victorious banner of our Party – Leninism! (*Tumultuous prolonged applause ending in ovation. All rise.*)

Krushchev's speech to the Twentieth Congress of the Communist Party, 25 February 1956

B A Later Critique Of Stalinism

The administrative command system . . . affected the whole political and social life of the country. Firmly established in the economy, it also spread to the superstructure, limiting the development of the democratic potential of socialism and restraining the progress of socialist democracy. . . . Methods imposed during the period of struggle against the hostile opposition of the exploiting classes were mechanically transferred to the period of peaceful socialist construction, when conditions had changed fundamentally. An atmosphere of intolerance, enmity and suspicion was created in the country. . . .

All this had a pernicious influence on the social and political development of the country, with serious consequences. It is extremely obvious that the absence of an adequate level of democratisation of Soviet society also made possible both the cult of the individual and the violations of legality, the arbitrariness and the repressions of the 1930s.

Report by M. Gorbachev on the Seventieth Anniversary of the Bolshevik Revolution, 2 November 1987

C The Thaw

THE STATUE'S SUNDERED PLINTH

The statue's sundered plinth is being smashed,
The steel of drills is sending up a howl.
The special hardset mixture of cement
Was calculated to endure millennia.
The time for re-evaluation came so soon.
And the present lesson is quite obvious:
Excessive concentration on eternity
Brings no advantage, we can justly say.
But these strong stones have such a deadly hold,
We have to sweat to force them break apart.
Excessive concentration on oblivion
Requires no small amount of labour too.
All handmade things in the world we live in
Can be reduced to scrap by hands of men.
But the main point is this:
Stone in its essence can
Be never either good or bad.

Alexander Tvardovsky (written after the removal of Stalin's body from the Lenin Mausoleum in 1962)

Questions

1 'Krushchev had no objection in principle to Stalin's methods – his only concern was how they were applied and against whom.' To what extent is this an accurate reading of Source A? **(10 marks)**

2 Compare and contrast the arguments used by the authors of Sources A and B. **(8 marks)**

3 a) Summarise the message of the poet in Source C. **(6 marks)**
  b) Can a poem like Source C be of value to an historian? You should refer to the Source in your answer. **(6 marks)**

4 Using Sources A–C, and your own knowledge, assess the validity of Deutscher's claim that 1956 marked 'a deep and radical break' in Soviet domestic policy. **(10 marks)**

5 FOREIGN POLICY IN THE KRUSHCHEV ERA

Krushchev inherited a difficult situation in foreign affairs. The USSR was 'contained' by a system of American-dominated alliances; and whilst the Soviets were anxious to reduce the clear military superiority enjoyed by the USA, overt action entailed risks and considerable expense.

Developments in the mid–1950s appeared to strengthen the Soviet position: the USSR acquired the H-bomb, successfully tested an ICBM and launched Sputnik, the first orbiting satellite. Krushchev was then prepared to formulate a policy of peaceful coexistence. In effect he stated that War, previously held to be an inevitable outcome of hostility between the Communist and Capitalist worlds, was now avoidable; not only would nuclear war be suicidal, it was unnecessary since Socialism would triumph over Capitalism by demonstrating its economic and social superiority.

Unfortunately for Krushchev, he faced problems elsewhere. The Chinese were no longer prepared to accept the USSR as leader of the world Communist movement, and thereafter Krushchev was perceived as a 'bourgeois revisionist'. Attempts to extend Soviet influence in the Third World met a mixed response. The Soviets could take advantage of the legacy of anti-imperialist feeling in the Middle East, Asia and Africa, and aid and trade agreements were forthcoming; but competition came from the Chinese, the Russians were sometimes seen as arrogant imperialists themselves, and it proved difficult to establish lasting influence.

Krushchev failed to avoid direct and dangerous confrontation with the USA. Attempts to alter the status of Berlin, achieve a disarmament agreement and reorganise the United Nations proved fruitless. Above all, the decision to counteract American superiority by establishing a bridgehead in Castro's Cuba almost brought the world to war and led to what was regarded in the USSR as a humiliating rebuff from the USA. There were some positive results to emerge from the Cuban Missiles Crisis, such as the Test Ban Treaty and the hot-line; however, of at least equal significance at the time, it was evident that Krushchev had embarked upon a policy of dangerous confrontation and had then been forced to withdraw.

By the time of Krushchev's fall from grace in 1964 there was little evidence of unity in the world Communist movement, and his attempts to attain strategic parity with the USA had obviously failed. At the time, these setbacks seemed more significant than his claims that the

Socialist world was now powerful enough to make war avoidable and that peaceful coexistence could be regarded as a permanent state of affairs.

A Peaceful Coexistence
Peaceful Coexistence of States with Different Social Systems: a form of the struggle waged between the opposite social systems in the world arena.

P.C. is rotted in socio-economic causes and is objectively necessary because socialism does not win simultaneously in all or even in the leading capitalist countries, and because capitalism, in turn, cannot engage in an incessant battle against the states where socialism has triumphed. P.C. of socialist and capitalist countries is, therefore, historically inevitable and not subject to the will of men. In the final analysis, it is a result of a balance of power between the two embattled systems that makes war hopeless for the bourgeoisie. The latter, by force of its social nature as a class basing its sway on violence and suppression, tries to resolve international conflicts by means of war, and only the growth of the forces of socialism and progress and, in the final count, their fundamental superiority, make it possible to neutralise this striving and exclude from international practice a world war and every type of unjust war. . . .

The chief goal set in the policy of P.C. is to preclude a new world war, which is, with the present level of destructive weapons, a major earnest of social progress and the attainment of socialism and communism. A nuclear war would not only take an enormous toll of human life and inflict immeasurable suffering on mankind, it would also bring in its wake, and precisely in the world's most developed states, the destruction of society's economic foundation, a huge devastation of the productive forces. . . .

The policy of P.C. is called on to create the conditions conducive to mass revolutionary movements; to enhance socialism's political authority and economic might, and hence its revolutionary impact; and to activate the working people's class struggle in the capitalist countries, and the national liberation movement. . . .

To realise the policy of P.C. it is very important to enhance mutually beneficial economic, scientific and cultural ties between states with different social systems in every possible way. The benefit gained by individual capitalists or capitalist countries from such ties cannot, of course, prevent or noticeably slow down the general decay of the capitalist system resulting from the aggravation of inherent contradictions. . . .

The principle and policy of P.C. are constantly attacked and criticised by both the most aggressive part of the monopoly bourgeoisie and petty-bourgeois revolutionaries, who are in no position to understand that socialism's political superiority in the world would gradually exclude coercion from international relations, rather than unleash an armed struggle against the capitalist system, and would finally lead to the total elimination of international armed conflicts. . . .

The CPSU and the international communist movement regard P.C. as a form of the class struggle under way in international politics, economics and ideology.

From *A Dictionary Of Scientific Communism* (Moscow 1980)

B Krushchev On Peaceful Coexistence
Our desire for peace and peaceful coexistence is not prompted by any time-serving or tactical considerations. It springs from the very nature of socialist society in which there are no classes or social groups interested in profiting by means of war or by seizing and enslaving foreign territories. . . . The main thing is to keep to the sphere of ideological struggle. . . . In our day there are only two ways, peaceful coexistence or the most destructive war in history. There is no third way.

Speech By Krushchev, 1959

C Further Thoughts From Krushchev
. . . There exist two camps in the world today, each with a different social system. The countries in these camps shape their policies along entirely different lines. In these circumstances, the problem of peaceful coexistence – that is, of safeguarding the world against the disaster of a military conflict between these two essentially antagonistic systems, between the groups of countries in which the two systems reign supreme – is of paramount importance. It is necessary to see to it that the inevitable struggle between them resolves solely into a struggle between ideologies and into peaceful emulation, or competition, to use a term that the capitalists find easier to understand. Each side will demonstrate its advantages to the best of its ability, but war as a means of settling this dispute must be ruled out. This, then, is coexistence as we Communists see it. . . .

Some Western politicians . . . misrepresent our aims because they are afraid of the influence which the peace policy of the socialist countries exerts on the peoples. We have never said, of course, that our aim is to conquer the world or a part of it. What does 'conquer' mean? It means forcibly to impose one's terms, one's political system, one's ideology, on the other side. But then that is not coexistence, it is interference in the internal affairs of other countries, it is war. It is something we are most emphatically opposed to. . . . The

Communists are firmly convinced that no ideology, including Communist ideology, can be implanted forcibly, by war, by bayonets. . . .

No bayonets, no prisons or force, can stem the ideas of Communism, for the simple reason that Marxism-Leninism is an expression of the vital interests of the working people, that it is the truth. . . . Communism will win, but not in the sense that the socialist countries will conquer the other countries. No, the people of each country will themselves weigh all the facts and when they have appreciated the essence of Marxism-Leninism, they will of their own free will choose the more progressive social system.

Report by Krushchev to the Supreme Soviet, 14 January 1960

D A Soviet View Of The Cuban Crisis

Who gave the United States the right to assume the role of ruler of the *destinies* of other countries and peoples? Why must the Cubans conduct the internal affairs of their country not as they see fit but as the United States prefers? Cuba belongs to the Cuban people and only it can be the master of its fate. . . . In this anxious hour the Soviet government considers itself duty-bound to seriously warn the government of the United States that in carrying out the measures announced by President Kennedy, it is recklessly playing with fire and taking a grave responsibility for the fate of the world. . . .

Who believes that Cuba can threaten the United States? If the size, resources and weapons of both countries are compared, no statesman in his right mind could see Cuba as a threat to the United States or to any other country. . . .

The United States has stopped at nothing, not even the organisation of the armed attack on Cuba of April 1961, to deprive the Cuban people of the freedom and independence it had won . . . and to make Cuba an American puppet.

Statement by the Soviet Government, 23 October 1962

E Krushchev Recalls The Crisis

We sent the Americans a note saying that we agreed to remove our missiles and bombers on the condition that the President give us his assurance that there would be no invasion of Cuba by the forces of the United States or anybody else. Finally Kennedy gave in and agreed to make a statement giving us such an assurance. . . . It has been, to say the least, an interesting and challenging situation. The two most powerful nations of the world had been squared off against each other, each with its finger on the button. . . . It was a great victory for us though . . . a triumph of Soviet foreign policy . . . a spectacular success without having to fire a single shot! . . . We behaved with dignity and forced the United States to demobilise and to recognise Cuba. . . . Cuba still exists today as a result of the correct policy conducted by the Soviet Union when it rebuffed the United States. I'm proud of what we did.

N. Krushchev: *Krushchev Remembers* (1971)

Questions

1 Using Source A, and your own knowledge, explain why the USSR adopted the policy of Peaceful Coexistence. **(8 marks)**

2 Was Krushchev's perception of Peaceful Coexistence in Sources B and C an accurate reflection of its analysis in Source A? Explain your answer. **(8 marks)**

3 Using your own knowledge, explain the circumstances which led the Soviet Government to issue the statement in Source D. **(6 marks)**

4 a) How does Krushchev justify his behaviour in the Cuban Crisis in Source E? **(4 marks)**

   b) Can Source E be considered a reliable source for an historian of this event? **(4 marks)**

5 Using Sources B–E, and your own knowledge, assess the validity of the claim that Krushchev's foreign policy was simply 'a continuation of Stalinism'. **(10 marks)**

6 BREZHNEV'S RUSSIA

Leonid Brezhnev was appointed General Secretary of the Party in 1965, following Krushchev's fall from power. Brezhnev was part of a collective leadership but, following an inter-party power struggle, he emerged as master of the Party and domestic affairs, whilst Kosygin was responsible for foreign affairs. By the mid–1970s all his leading rivals were either dead or demoted; and, whilst Brezhnev preferred to govern through consensus, until his death in 1982 he was effectively the dominant voice in the USSR, head of both Party and Government, and with his own 'personality cult'. In many respects it was a period of stagnation in domestic affairs, when much-needed reforms were neglected and problems ignored. Brezhnev's successors were to reap an unfortunate harvest.

Brezhnev demonstrated a similar interest in agriculture to his old master Krushchev. State investment in agriculture was increased, agricultural administration was reformed and the peasants were given more incentives. However, yields remained disappointingly low. In industry, despite the exploitation of Siberia and investment programmes in the republics, growth rates declined sharply after 1975. The economy was stagnating through factors such as bureaucratic inefficiency, over-centralisation, lack of investment, poor labour productivity and the demands of the defence sector. Although real wages rose in the 1970s, shortages in housing and consumer goods continued. Many critics see the Brezhnev era as the 'lost years', when the old Stalinist economic and social order was allowed to continue whilst some other countries improved their status in relative terms.

The Brezhnev Constitution of 1977 confirmed, or even increased, the official rights of Soviet citizens, but also reiterated the leading role of the Party. The Party contained a high proportion of relatively new members, and maintained its hold on all areas of Soviet life. In the same month as Brezhnev's death, it was announced that the next year's target for industrial growth would be the lowest figure since 1929: the Soviet people paid a high price for the priority given to defence spending and the accompanying stagnation, a price which was to force Brezhnev's successors into a reappraisal of the very foundations of the Soviet system.

A Brezhnev Considers The Future

In recent years negative phenomena have appeared, such as a slowing down of the rates of growth of production and labour productivity and a reduction in the effectiveness of the utilisation of production assets and capital investments. Unless we adopt a critical approach we cannot give a correct appraisal, without which our advance will be less successful. . . . The rates of economic growth were affected by shortcomings in administration and planning, by underestimation of the methods of economic accountability and by failure to make full use of material and moral incentives. . . .

First of all, it is necessary to say that the five-year plan for 1966–70 is an important new stage in the Soviet people's struggle to create the material and technical base of communism. The CPSU Central Committee defined the *chief task* of the new five-year plan. It is *to ensure – on the basis of the comprehensive utilisation of the achievements of science and technology, the industrial development of all social production and a rise in its effectiveness and in the productivity of labour – the further significant growth of industry and a high stable rate of agricultural development, and thereby to attain a substantial rise in the people's standard of living and the fuller satisfaction of the material and cultural needs of all Soviet people.*

Brezhnev's report to the Twenty-Third Congress of the Communist Party, 29 March 1966

B Kosygin Promises A Better Life

In the new five-year period, our people's material well-being will increase first of all as a result of increases in the wages and salaries of workers and office employees and in the incomes of collective farmers in step with growing labour productivity and the improved skills of personnel. This will provide the bulk of the increment in the population's incomes. . . .

. . . The minimum wage will be raised . . . the minimum size of the old-age pension for workers and office employees will be increased . . . market supplies of such products as meat, fish, vegetable oil, eggs and vegetables will increase by 40 per cent to 60 per cent. . . . We must substantially increase the production of packaged goods and develop the practice of advance orders, mail trade and other progressive trade forms. Provision has been made for at least doubling the volume of *everyday services* to the population. . . . *Housing construction* will to an increasing extent be carried out. . . . It is necessary to devote great attention to improving communal services and the provision of communities with public services and amenities. . . . We shall *complete the introduction of universal secondary education.*

Kosygin's report on the Five-Year Plan, 6 April 1971

C A Programme For The 1980s
The crux of the Party's economic strategy is expressed in the basic target for the 1981–5 period – further to raise the well being of the Soviet people on the basis of the steady development of the national economy, accelerated scientific and technological progress, the transfer of the economy to an intensive path of development, economising on all resources and raising the quality of work. It was also planned to increase the output and raise the quality of consumer goods and extend the services offered to the population.

Report of the Twenty-Sixth Congress of the Communist Party, February–March 1981

D The New Constitution
The draft of the new Constitution also states that *a developed socialist society has been created in the USSR and that the supreme goal of the Soviet state is the building of Communism*. It is emphasised that *our state is a state of all the people and* that it expresses the will and interests of the working class, the peasantry and the intelligentsia, of all the country's nations and nationalities. . . .

The draft gives significantly fuller formulation to *the political rights and liberties of USSR citizens*. . . . Freedom of speech, of the press, of assembly, of mass meetings and of street processions and demonstrations, which are included in the Constitution now in effect, are restated in full. . . .

Needless to say, comrades, the draft Constitution proceeds from the premise that the rights and liberties of citizens cannot and must not be used against our social system or to the detriment of the Soviet people's interests. Therefore, the draft clearly states, for example, that the exercise by citizens of their rights and liberties must not injure the interests of society and the state or the rights of other citizens and that political liberties are granted in accordance with the working people's interests and for the purpose of strengthening the socialist system.

Report by Brezhnev to the Central Committee, 'On The Draft Constitution Of The USSR' 24 May 1977

E Developed Socialism
The working class is the decisive force in laying the material and technical foundations of communism. It is numerically the largest class of socialist society, and its main productive force. The key positions the working class occupies in the socialist economy, its revolutionary spirit, organisation, collectivism, discipline, political consciousness and active participation in running state and social affairs determine

its leading position in the USSR, which it retains right until communism has been built.

Important progressive changes are under way within the peasantry. The collective farmer of today has grown up under socialism, which has shaped his character, ideological views and moral qualities. The collective farmers are closer than ever to the urban working people in their educational level, working conditions, remuneration for labour, the level of consumption, and the way of life.

The Soviet intelligentsia is now playing a greater role in the building of communism, which is a direct result of the people's cultural advancement. . . .

M. Suslov, Secretary Of The CPSU Central Committee,
'Marxism–Leninism And The Revolutionary Renovation Of The World'
(Moscow, 1977)

F The Food Crisis
It has become obvious that extensive factors for growth in agro-industrial production have been virtually exhausted. . . .
Organisational disarray developed: several specialised subdivisions performing the same type of work were set up in each district. . . .
Confusion in the material and technical supply of collective farms and state farms has become appreciable. . . . Local agencies saw . . . breakdowns in coordination but were unable to eliminate them because they lacked the authority to replicate the investments among enterprises of different departments and could not manoeuvre resources as they needed to.

V. Miloserdov: 'New Stage In The Management Of The Agro-Industrial Complex' in *Pravda*, 6 August 1982

G Some Concerns of the Regime

(i) 'My loving care and attention will help me farm!' 1971 poster.

(ii) 'Our hopes and deeds belong to Mother Russia and the Party!' 1976 poster.

(iii) 'Grain to the Motherland.' 1978 poster.

(iv) 'We are the young working class!' 1975 poster.

ДОРОГУ В БУДУЩЕЕ ПРОЛОЖИМ!

(v) 'We are forging the future!' 1977 poster.

Questions

1 Using your own knowledge, and Sources A, B and C, consider the extent to which the Soviet economy succeeded by 1982 in fulfilling the hopes expressed in the Sources. **(10 marks)**

2 How democratic was the Constitution outlined in Source D?
(6 marks)

3 Using your own knowledge of the period, explain the extent to which the claims made in Sources D and E were realised in practice.
(7 marks)

4 Use Source F and your own knowledge to explain why agriculture had been a problem for the Soviet Government since the Second World War. **(8 marks)**

5 Study Source G:
   a) What concerns of the regime are expressed in these posters?
(6 marks)
   b) How do the posters attempt to convey their message? **(6 marks)**
   c) How reliable are these posters as historical evidence? **(6 marks)**

7 A GLOBAL STRATEGY AND DETENTE

During the late 1960s and 1970s Soviet foreign policy continued some of the themes of the Krushchev years: striving for parity with the USA and attempting to consolidate the Socialist bloc and world Communist movement. The degree of success was mixed. By the time of Brezhnev's death in 1982, the USSR was a global Superpower, but it was over-extended in its commitments, was entrenched in an unpopular war in Afghanistan, and its efforts at Detente had failed.

In the 1960s defence spending rose steadily, with particular emphasis upon enhancing the navy as an instrument of global policy. By the 1970s the Soviets had finally equalled, if not surpassed, the USA in terms of strategic parity and were willing to pursue a policy of Detente, or relaxation of international tension. However, such an approach encountered opposition from conservatives within the USSR, and it was emphasised that the ideological struggle with the capitalist world must continue.

The SALT I Agreements of the early 1970s produced a measure of arms control and paved the way for bilateral agreements with several countries. However, further progress towards disarmament or arms control was hampered by the West's insistence on linking such measures with issues of human rights. Developments in weaponry and existing suspicions between the Superpowers were simply heightened by the Soviet invasion of Afghanistan in 1979.

The Brezhnev era saw continued Soviet efforts to extend influence in the Third World: Vietnam, Angola, Somalia, Ethiopia, the Arab States and India. South America was difficult to penetrate. Success in all these areas was limited. With regard to economics the Soviets could not compete with the Americans, and military influence did not always readily translate into political influence. Soviet influence in the Eastern bloc was maintained, notably in Czechoslovakia in 1968; yet the uncompromising Brezhnev Doctrine, with its insistence on the right of Soviet intervention in the Socialist camp, did not disguise the fact that Eastern Europe was gradually becoming less dependent upon the USSR. Even without the worldwide condemnation inspired by the invasion of Afghanistan, Soviet efforts to create and maintain a global strategy had only limited success, particularly considering the connection between defence and internal economic strains.

A The Brezhnev Doctrine

A) There is no doubt that the peoples of the socialist countries and the Communist Parties have and must have freedom to determine their country's path to development. However, any decision of theirs must damage neither socialism in their own country nor the fundamental interests of other socialist countries. . . . This means that every Communist Party is responsible not only to its own people but also to all the socialist countries and the entire Communist movement. Whoever forgets this is placing sole emphasis on the autonomy and independence of Communist Parties, lapses into onesidedness, shirking his internationalist obligations. . . . Just as, in V. I. Lenin's words, someone living in a system of other states constituting a socialist commonwealth cannot be free of the common interests of that commonwealth.

S. Kovalev: 'Sovereignty And The International Obligations Of Communist Countries' in *Pravda*, 26 September 1968

B) When internal and external forces hostile to socialism attempt to turn the development of any socialist country in the direction of the capitalist system . . . it already becomes not only a problem for the people of that country, but also a general problem, the concern of all socialist countries.

Declaration by Brezhnev, November 1968

B Detente

The Union of Soviet Socialist Republics and the United States of America . . . have agreed as follows:

First: They will proceed from the common determination that in the nuclear age there is no alternative to conducting their mutual relations on the basis of peaceful coexistence. Differences in ideology and in the social systems of the USSR and the USA are not obstacles to the bilateral development of normal relations based on the principles of sovereignty, equality, non-interference in internal affairs and mutual advantage.

Second: The USSR and the USA . . . will do their utmost to avoid military confrontations and to prevent the outbreak of nuclear war. They will always exercise restraint in their mutual relations, and will be prepared to negotiate and settle differences by peaceful means.

Third: The USSR and the USA have a special responsibility to do everything in their power so that conflicts or situations will not arise which would serve to increase international tensions. Accordingly, they will seek to promote conditions in which all countries will live in peace and security and will not be subject to outside interference in their internal affairs.

'Basic Principles Of Relations Between The USSR And The USA' signed in Moscow, 29 May 1972

C Brezhnev Reports On Progress
Struggle to consolidate the principles of peaceful coexistence, to assure lasting peace, to reduce, and in the longer term to eliminate, the danger of another world war has been, and remains, the main element of our policy toward the capitalist states. It may be noted that considerable progress has been achieved in this area in the last five years.

The passage from Cold War, from the explosive confrontation of the two worlds, to detente was primarily connected with changes in the correlation of world forces. But much effort was required for people – especially those responsible for the policy of states – to become accustomed to the thought that not brinkmanship but negotiation of disputed questions, not confrontation but peaceful cooperation, is the natural state of things. . . .

Though world peace is by no means guaranteed as yet, we have every reason to declare that the improvement of the international climate is convincing evidence that lasting peace is not merely a good intention, but an entirely realistic object. And we can and must continue to work tirelessly in the name of achieving it.

Report by Brezhnev at the Twenty-Fifth Congress of the Communist Party, 24 February 1976

D The End Of Detente?
In the late 1970s and early 1980s international relations once more became complicated and dangerously aggravated. Increasingly active were circles seeking to undermine and destroy the only possible basis of relations between states in an age of nuclear weapons. . . . These circles resented the improvement in international relations in the preceding decade and systematically attacked the process of detente. In the vanguard of the forces striving to direct world developments along a dangerous path, as their predecessors did in the first post-war years, was again the United States, or, to be more precise, the Republican Administration led by Ronald Reagan. . . .

US actions in the international arena in the early 1980s show that the United States has not only departed from the policy of detente, but has also failed to honour agreements and treaties, ignoring centuries-old standards of international law. Washington has in effect wrecked the 1979 Soviet-US treaty on limiting strategic armaments (SALT–2), a treaty which took years of hard work to prepare and which equally considers the real interests of both countries. The United States also withdrew from a whole series of negotiations on important problems of ending the arms race and from talks that were making good headway or were nearing a successful completion.

V. Nekrasov: *The Roots Of European Security* (Moscow, 1984)

E Intervention In Afghanistan

... Developments forced us to make a choice: we had either to bring in troops or let the Afghan revolution be defeated and the country turned into a kind of Shah's Iran. We decided to bring in the troops. It was not a simple decision to take. We weighed the pros and cons before taking it. We knew that the victory of counter-revolution and of religious zealots and revenge-seeking feudal lords would result in a bloodbath before which even the crimes of the Chilean junta would pale. We knew that the victory of counter-revolution would pave the way for massive American military presence in a country which borders on the Soviet Union and that this was a challenge to our country's security. We knew that the decision to bring in troops would not be popular in the modern world even if it was absolutely legal. But we also knew that we would have ceased to be a great power if we refrained from carrying the burden of taking unpopular but necessary decisions, extraordinary decisions prompted by extraordinary circumstances. ... There are situations when non-intervention is a disgrace and a betrayal. Such a situation developed in Afghanistan. And when I hear the voices of protest from people who claim to be democrats, humanists and even revolutionaries, saying they are outraged by Soviet 'intervention' I tell them this: it is logic that prompted us. If you are against Soviet military aid to Afghanistan, then you are for the victory of counter-revolution. There is no third way.

A. Bovin in *Izvestia*, April 1980

F The Propaganda War

(i) 1980s peace propaganda.

(ii) 1980s peace propaganda.

(iii) 1980s peace propaganda.

(iv) 1980s peace propaganda.

(v) 1980s propaganda, 'Guiding star'.

(vi) 'America – 1983'.

Questions

1 What justification for Soviet intervention in other countries is given in Source A? **(5 marks)**

2 Using your own knowledge, explain the circumstances which existed in Eastern Europe in 1968 which led to the arguments in Source A being put forward. **(5 marks)**

3 Using Source B, and your own knowledge, explain the circumstances which led to Detente in the 1970s. **(7 marks)**

4 a) Compare and contrast Sources B, C and D in their interpretation of Superpower relations in the 1970s. **(8 marks)**
b) Account for any differences in tone between the Sources. **(5 marks)**

5 For what reasons, according to Source E, did the USSR invade Afghanistan? **(5 marks)**

6 a) Identify the principal themes of the propaganda posters in Source F. **(6 marks)**
b) Compare and contrast the methods used in Source F to convey these themes. **(7 marks)**
c) Which of these posters would be of most use to an historian, and why? **(6 marks)**

7 To what extent do Sources A–F demonstrate a consistent line in Soviet policy during the Brezhnev era? **(10 marks)**

8 THE GORBACHEV ERA

Although Brezhnev had favoured Konstantin Chernenko as his successor, following the former's death in 1982, it was the reformist ex-head of the KGB, Yuri Andropov, who was nominated as the General Secretary. Andropov lived for little more than a year after his appointment: during that time he initiated some of the reforms later associated with Gorbachev, and encountered some of the conservative resistance which was to reappear on a larger scale. Chernenko then held office between Andropov's death in February 1984 and his own demise in March 1985.

Mikhail Gorbachev was politically of the post-Stalinist, post-war generation, and represented the technocrat, reforming, non-corruptible breed of Party man. On his succession as General Secretary he soon showed his political skills in promoting like-minded colleagues, such as Foreign Minister Shevardnadze, and retiring several old Brezhnevites from the Politburo or other influential positions.

Establishing his pre-eminence in the hierarchy proved easier than enforcing change in the middle ranks of the Government and Party machines, where Party careerists and officials were often fearful for their own security and therefore suspicious of reform.

Gorbachev's problem was to maintain a balance between alienating the still powerful conservative forces in Soviet society and losing the goodwill of the many people in the lower levels of society who were willing to support the proposed changes – changes symbolised in the campaigns of *Glasnost* and *Perestroika*. By 1991 Gorbachev appeared to be allowing Conservative elements to prevail again, as nationalist movements in the Baltic states came under ideological and actual physical attack. Foreign Minister Shevardnadze resigned in protest at the movement to the Right, and there were increasing doubts as to how far Gorbachev was actually in control of the political process.

The stagnation of the Brezhnev years proved difficult to reverse. Low agricultural yields remained a perennial problem; efforts to improve productivity and quality through industrial reorganisation ran into problems; Glasnost revealed a host of social problems previously wholly or partly hidden; nationalist stirrings within and without the Soviet Empire threatened Gorbachev's very survival.

Whilst remaining a very powerful body within the USSR, by 1990 the Communist Party had lost the monopoly position it had enjoyed since shortly after the Revolution. Elections are now contested, although independent candidates do face difficulties. The Supreme Soviet became a genuinely legislative body. Yet despite these reforms, the President was facing serious difficulties. In 1990 his populist rival Boris Yeltsin was elected as President of the Russian Federation and made radical promises such as a multi-party government and the establishment of Russian sovereignty within the Soviet Union. Popular dissatisfaction with Gorbachev grew as economic reforms appeared to have failed.

Some analysts perceived great skill in Gorbachev's attempts to steer a course between extreme Left and Right; some doubted his ability to survive long. What was certainly true by the beginning of the new decade was that Gorbachev's reputation was proving easier to uphold abroad than it was amongst a more cynical population at home.

A The Brezhnev Legacy

Brezhnev was an obedient aide. Nobody took him seriously as a challenger for the General Secretaryship and he himself bent over backwards to show he had no such ambitions. . . . The choice of Brezhnev followed the pattern prevalent in local Party branches, where, instead of choosing the most active, daring and competent man to be Secretary, the members opt for the most reliable man, who will never let anybody down or do anyone any harm. . . . At sessions of the Central Committee Secretariat or Praesidium he did not usually speak first. He would let everybody else state their opinions and if, in the end, there was no consensus, he would put off the final decision, talk to everybody again, find common ground, and then call another session. It was under Brezhnev that there emerged the practice of multi-stage agreement of resolutions, demanding dozens of signatures on even a minor document, as a result of which the final decision got either bogged down or distorted. . . .

So Brezhnev came to power without any specific programme for national development. . . . Being highly conservative by nature, what he feared most of all was any sudden change. Having condemned Krushchev's subjectivism, the first thing he did was to reverse Krushchev's radical reforms and reinstate Stalin's tried and tested methods. . . . The high-ranking officials who had been sent to work in outlying areas much to their displeasure, now returned to their cushy jobs in Moscow. Quietly, the idea of rotation of jobs for officials was also shelved. Instead, the slogan of the day was stability – the dream of any *apparatchik*. . . .

It was Brezhnev who started the tradition of empty speechifying. . . . The Soviet taxpayer paid for everything. Who is to say how many billions of roubles and how many tons of young people's enthusiasm was wasted on the economically unjustified Baikal-Amur main line project? And how much scientific brain-power was wasted on the grandiose idea of reversing the Siberian rivers? And how much public money was squandered on the arms drive? In the meantime the people's living standards plummeted to the bottom of the list of industrialised nations. . . .

Brezhnev presided over two decades of lost opportunities. The high-technology revolution had knocked on the door, but no one had answered. . . . True, the Soviet Union reached military parity with the United States. But that was done at the cost of increased technological backwardness in the rest of the economy, continued disintegration of agriculture, failing to build a modern service sector, and the freezing of low living standards.

Matters were compouded by the fact that the Party rejected any attempts to update socialism. It believed only in administrative solutions. . . . The most important lesson that we should learn from the Brezhnev period is that the command administration style of management that took shape under Stalin does not work. The state, far from promoting progress, was becoming more and more of a drag on society – economically, culturally, and morally. . . . The only way out is development of a truly democratic socialist society based on self-governing economic entities and active individuals. . . . The second lesson is that we must tolerate no longer a system under which leaders come to power through backstage intrigues or bloody purges instead of a normal democratic procedure. . . . We need to see all candidates for higher posts in public life and, of course, we need a truly democratic electoral procedure. . . .

F. Burlatsky: 'A Hero Of Times Past' in *Literaturnaya Gazeta* (Moscow 1988)

B The Gorbachev Analysis

We act according to Lenin . . . which means to study how the future grows out of the present-day reality and to map out our plans accordingly. . . . The renewal of developing socialism is a process which goes beyond the turn of the century. . . . Of everlasting importance is the fact that Marxism, developing the ideas of socialism, represented socialism as the natural product of the progress of civilisation. . . .

As we delve deeper into the essence of our own history, it becomes increasingly clear that the October Revolution was not an error – and not only because a realistic alternative to it was by no means a bourgeois democratic republic, as some people now try to make us believe – but an anarchic mutiny, a bloody dictatorship of the military and the establishment of a reactionary anti-popular regime. . . .

At the present complex stage, the interests of the consolidation of society and the concentration of all its sound forces on the difficult tasks of perestroika prompt the advisability of keeping the one-party system. . . . The socialism to which we advance during perestroika means a society based on an effective economy, on the highest achievements of science, technology, and culture, and on the humanised social structures.

M. Gorbachev in *Pravda*, 26 November 1989

C 'Unofficial' Demands For Change

As convinced proponents of socialism, we support the goal of moving towards a classless society and the complete withering away of the state, which was proclaimed in October 1917. . . . We acknowledge the constitutional role of the Communist Party of the Soviet Union in our society, but the party is not united. Its ranks include those who bear responsibility for the abuses and miscalculations of the past. . . . We aim to support the healthy and progressive forces in the party's leadership and the rank and file. . . .

The Federation's aims are the following:
In the ideological field: to work out a conception of democracy for our society, to solve the dialectical contradiction between administrative power and social self-management. . . .
In the political field: to work out a legal status for independent organisations and movements, giving them the right to make proposals for legislation . . . to democratise the electoral system. . . .
In the economic field: to reorientate the organs of state planning and management from primarily administrative methods to economic ones . . . to switch the economy to self-management . . . to democratise the planning system. . . .
In the cultural field: to allow creative associations to operate freely on a self-financing basis; to provide a climate of tolerance for all creative public attitudes and tastes of whatever direction, provided they do not contradict the constitution of the USSR. . . .
In the ecological field: . . . to fight for the conservation of the environment, as well as historical and cultural monuments.
In the field of international relations: to show support and solidarity to revolutionary, liberation and democratic movements in the capitalist world and in developing countries.

Manifesto of the Federation of Socialist Clubs (Moscow, August 1987)

Questions

1 Using your own knowledge, explain the references to Krushchev's reforms in Source A.   **(4 marks)**

2 To what extent does Source A help to explain Gorbachev's programme of reform? **(7 marks)**

3 Comment on the methods used by Gorbachev in Source B to justify his reform programme. **(5 marks)**

4 Compare and contrast Sources A, B and C in their analysis of how the USSR should develop. **(9 marks)**

5 To what extent had the demands made in these Sources been realised by the end of the 1980s? **(7 marks)**

9 THE LIMITATIONS OF POWER:

FOREIGN AFFAIRS IN THE GORBACHEV ERA

When he came to power Gorbachev did not initiate a fundamentally new foreign policy. He was, however, anxious to resurrect Detente: in order to reduce spending on defence and concentrate on domestic reform, Gorbachev required peace and agreements with the West. One advantage which he possessed over his predecessors was skill in presentation and public relations which won him considerable goodwill abroad.

The early signs were not encouraging: Gorbachev inherited the problem of Afghanistan; relations with the USA were soured by Reagan's 'Star Wars' plans; and a Soviet moratorium on nuclear testing and disarmament proposals achieved little positive response from Western governments, whatever their impact upon public opinion. However, some success was achieved in 1987 when negotiations on 'Star Wars' were separated from other issues, and the dismantling of short-range missiles in Europe finally began. The Cold War appeared to be almost over, assisted by the final withdrawal of troops from Afghanistan in 1989.

There were also significant changes in Soviet relations with Eastern Europe. Gorbachev explicitly encouraged reform in Eastern European states and announced the abandoning of the Brezhnev Doctrine. Undoubtedly his attitude stimulated the remarkable changes which took place in East Germany, Czechoslovakia, Romania and other former satellite states during 1989 and 1990.

Elsewhere Gorbachev continued existing trends in Soviet foreign policy. Links with friendly states in Africa and Asia were maintained. Soviet policy towards the Third World was already being reassessed when Gorbachev arrived in the Kremlin; the returns on previous efforts had not been great, and considerable expense had been incurred. Therefore Moscow decided to concentrate more on the industrialising capitalist states.

Soviet foreign policy has usually been pragmatic in approach and ideological considerations have rarely been a determining factor. Gorbachev's particular contribution was to recognise the fact that the USSR had probably already passed its peak as a world power. Competition with the USA was to give way to cooperation: competition simply harmed the USSR economically and heightened international tension. Hence the radical disarmament proposals discussed at the

Bush-Gorbachev summit off Malta in December 1989 and the apparent willingness of the USSR to cooperate with the West during the Iraq crisis in the summer of 1990. Gorbachev faced great problems, for example in persuading the Soviet military establishment to his world view; and the future direction of foreign policy would be affected by economic and political factors, including the outcome of debates over the very structure of the Soviet Union itself. The decreasing influence of the USSR as a superpower was demonstrated by her ineffectual role in the war against Iraq early in 1991. History as yet must suspend its assessment of Gorbachev as either a determined realist or a misguided utopian.

A A Foreign Minister Speaks His Mind

A country's foreign policy is viable only when it bases itself on the law, on convictions, on compatible interests and targets, on cooperation and interaction. The policy of using military power to underpin diplomacy always drove states to political bankruptcy or catastrophe. Great empires collapsed, while states which have practically no armed forces flourish.

Foreign policy can only achieve limited objectives. If we go back to 1917, we see that many people in Britain, France, or the United States asked indignantly how and why their governments had permitted the Revolution in Russia to prevail. . . .

Of late we have seen the appearance of a similar type of accuser in our country. One gets the impression that some would have wanted to launch a detailed investigation into 'who lost Eastern Europe?'

I feel pain and bitterness when I see some people who reason that the Soviet army, far from liberating some European countries, actually seized them as war trophies. . . .

Foreign policy, like domestic policy, cannot defend and protect the indefensible; situations that contradict generally accepted views on equality, freedom and people's power, or developments that go against the natural course of history. . . . When we talk about ridding inter-state relations from ideological confrontation we have in mind the need to liberate foreign policies from deformed ideology, and from ideological extremism.

'Is there a future for the Warsaw Pact organisation?' I am asked. The Pact has not always been there. It was set up in 1955. NATO was set up in 1949. . . . As with any other agreement, the Warsaw Treaty is not an eternal thing. . . . The trouble is that our organisation turned out to be resistant to change, and did not always keep pace with circumstances. There was a failure to modernise and adapt its military and political structures. . . . When we look at what is happening with the Warsaw Treaty and at the revolutionary events in Eastern Europe, we can learn the same lesson: durable policies can only be achieved if they are supported by the will of people and states.

What reply is there for those who challenge us to explain why we permitted changes in Eastern Europe, or why we agreed to withdraw our troops from there? These critics seem to imply that we should have used tanks to 'bring about order'. Can anyone seriously believe that the problem can be solved by such methods?

It is obvious that some aspects of our foreign policy are not being carried out in the best way; some are handled very badly. But serious criticism should not stop at questions why this or the other had not been done. Criticism has to be thought through to its logical conclusion.

Setting aside the moral and legal aspects, the course advocated by our critics would lead to a sharp deterioration of Soviet relations with other countries, to conflicts or even wars. Everyone who advocates a policy of military interventionism should address themselves to those young men who will be sent into combat, and to their mothers.

It is time we understood that neither socialism, nor friendship, nor good neighbourliness, nor respect can rely on bayonets, tanks and bloodshed. Relations with any country must be built on mutual interests, mutual advantage, on the principle of free choice. . . .

Some of our critics are suggesting that the troop withdrawals from Hungary, Czechoslovakia, Poland, Mongolia and East Germany were decided without reference to, and against the will of, the military.

This is not true. At all times, our army colleagues participated in our policy discussions. . . .

Let me explain the mechanism of the disarmament negotiations. Our delegations are made up of all the interested departments on an equal basis. Generals and colonels and other officers take part, as well as representatives of the military industries. The place where our positions are agreed and negotiating directives worked out – I am revealing a secret here – is in the General Staff. . . .

We are supposed to be in an era of *glasnost*. People criticise the diplomats for unspecified concessions which have allegedly harmed our security. Is it not time to speak about security more openly? Soviet taxpayers have a right to know what security they are getting for their money.

Article by Foreign Minister Shevardnadze in *Pravda* June 1990

Questions

1 Using your own knowledge, explain the references in Source A to 'lost Eastern Europe' and 'the revolutionary events in Eastern Europe.'

(8 marks)

2 Comment on the validity of the statement that this article represented 'a fundamental and revolutionary break with traditional Soviet foreign policy.' **(10 marks)**

10 CULTURAL DEVELOPMENTS

SINCE THE SECOND WORLD WAR

Cultural freedom in the Western liberal sense did not exist under Stalin. Socialist Realism continued as the prevailing philosophy after the War. The creative artist was to serve the ideological needs of the regime. In practice this meant: idealising the achievements of Socialism, particularly by creating stereotypes such as the heroic worker; considerable emphasis on the exploits of the War years; and an insistence on optimism, whatever the fate of individuals. Certain writers featured very heavily: for example the works of Gorky and Mayakovsky comprised half the school curriculum in literature. Theatre, cinema, television, radio and literature were all subject to censorship.

Krushchev's regime saw a partial cultural liberalisation; but, in 1966 the trial of the writers Daniel and Sinyavsky marked a reversion to stricter controls. Other individuals to suffer included Sakharov and Solzhenitsyn. However, educational and cultural standards were rising, and the demand for freer expression was met partly by the spread of underground literature and music.

A notable early feature of the Gorbachev reforms was a cultural thaw on an unprecedented scale. In the era of *Glasnost* it became possible to exhibit avant-guarde art and to write and compose more freely. The media was revitalised; cultural experiment was encouraged, and a mass of contained energy was finally released. A similarly liberal attitude toward the Church developed after years of persecution under Stalin (apart from during the War) and Krushchev. In 1990 censorship was officially abolished, a move condemned by Conservatives but welcomed by those Russians who saw freedom of cultural expression as an integral part of a move toward a pluralist society. Yet the liberalisation process was under attack from Conservatives again early in 1991.

A A Stalinist View of Culture

We demand that our comrades, both practising writers and those in positions of literary leadership, should be guided by that without which the Soviet order cannot live, that is to say, by politics, so that our young people may be brought up not in the spirit of 'do-nothing' and 'don't care', but in an optimistic and revolutionary spirit. . . . All the best representatives of the revolutionary democratic Russian intellectuals have denounced 'pure art' and 'art for art's sake', and have been the spokesmen of art for the people, demanding that art should have a worthy educational and social significance. . . .

However fine may be the external appearance of the work of fashionable modern bourgeois writers in America and Western Europe, and their film directors and theatrical producers, they can neither save nor better their bourgeois culture, for its moral basis is rotten and decaying. It has been placed at the service of capitalist private ownership, of the selfish and egocentric interests of the top layer of bourgeois society . . . treating of gangsters and showgirls and glorifying the adulterer and the adventures of crooks and gamblers.

Andrei Zhdanov, a leading Party ideologist, 1947

B A Cultural Overview From 1981

. . . The Communist Party of the Soviet Union and the Soviet Government strive to ensure that the best works of literature and art of all nations and times influence the shaping of the inner and spiritual world of Soviet people, the moulding of their moral principles and aesthetic tastes. Particular attention is paid to the development of Soviet culture. The work of the intellectual and artistic community in the Soviet Union is held in high esteem and the most favourable conditions have been provided to encourage their creative pursuits. . . .

Socialism has not only placed artistic and other spiritual values within the reach of the mass of the people, it has also made the people the direct creator of cultural values. The Soviet people's impressive achievements in the field of cultural activity are fresh proof of Lenin's words to the effect that only by winning freedom and national independence can working people obtain an unlimited opportunity to combat benightedness and ignorance and to enjoy the benefits of science and culture to the full.

Y. Kukushkin: *History Of The USSR* (Moscow 1981)

C Culture Under Glasnost
SOVIET FASCISM

Coming at once – the MILITIA!
At once – the MILITIA!
In our country they won't allow us to revolt!
Our country is a land of passions and dull bureaucrats!
OUR country – don't you dare produce Black COLONELS,
Who point the muzzles of their revolvers at us,
Who crush us with the rough force of cudgels.
Our rebellious country, God forbid that you
Should bend our people under the FASCIST BOOT!

Poem by the Moscow Arbat Street poet Violetta Anatolevna, 1989

D Some Cultural Concerns in the 1980s

(i) 1988 poster: 'In memory of the Seventeenth Congress of the Communist Party.' The majority of the delegates at the 1934 Congress were purged during the next three years. At the Congress, Stalin jokingly trained a hunting rifle (a gift) on the audience.

(ii) 1980s poster: 'My breadwinners' – A satire on the Orthodox Church.

(iii) 1980s poster: 'Where is the grill-bar here?'

(iv) 1980s poster: 'They gave him everything – from jeans to a bride. . . . But Vasca only hears what he wants'.

«КУЛЬТУРНЫЙ ОБМЕН»

Большой бизнесмен мистер Джон!
Во всем разбирается тонко —
И в ценности русских икон,
И в жалких запросах подонка.

(v) 1980s poster: 'Cultural exchange' – Black market operations were an everyday occurrence in Soviet life.

(vi) 1989 cartoon: 'Miss Muddleheaded' – Not everyone approved of capitalist influences.

Questions

1 Compare Sources A and B in their view of the role of culture and the artist in Soviet society. What identifies them as being from the pre-*Glasnost* era? **(8 marks)**

2 Study Source C. Could this poem have been published openly in the USSR before the era of *Glasnost*? Explain your answer. **(4 marks)**

3 Study the posters and pictures in Source D:
  a) Identify the cultural concerns demonstrated in these sources. **(6 marks)**

  b) In what ways are these concerns put across? **(6 marks)**
  c) Is there any evidence of *Glasnost* in these sources? **(6 marks)**
  d) Discuss the uses and limitations to an historian of any three of these sources. **(6 marks)**

11 PERESTROIKA

During the Brezhnev years the USSR experienced several difficulties. The slowdown in economic growth has already been described. In addition, the rate of population growth was declining, whilst the shift in the existing population from rural to urban areas continued. The Russians faced the prospect of being outnumbered by non-Russians, particularly with the greatest population growth taking place in the Muslim Republics.

Gorbachev realised the fundamental weaknesses in the Soviet economy and that at stake was the stability and prestige of the USSR and even the authority of the Party. Agricultural reform was one of the priorities: yields were too low and planning was inflexible. Thus schemes were introduced to improve incentives and output, in particular giving some autonomy to farmers. Industry was equally a problem. Modernisation, increased labour discipline, self-financing, more technology, more investment, freedom from central bureaucratic controls, worker incentives, rationalisation – all these measures were discussed and implemented to a greater or lesser degree between 1985 and 1990. A Fifteen Year Plan was to see the USSR through to the year 2000.

Initially this attempt at a fundamental restructuring of the economy, of *Perestroika*, was greeted with enthusiasm by many sections of the Soviet population, if not the Conservatives in the Party, on the assumption that the benefits would include considerable improvements in the quality and quantity of consumer goods. By the end of the 1980s this enthusiasm had largely turned to cynicism: not only were many people upset by calls for greater exertion and new deprivations – for example a reduction in the provision of alcohol and rationing of some goods – but many of the promised benefits had failed to materialise. The prospects of *Perestroika*, and even of Gorbachev's survival, seemed under threat. Conservatives blamed the whole concept, and claimed that the introduction of measures of limited private enterprise, particularly in the service sector, was simply surreptitious capitalism. Radicals maintained that failures were due to obstructionism by unsympathetic bureaucrats and the fact that reform simply did not go far enough; and that, for example, there had to be a complete overhaul of the pricing and subsidy system, together with more radical decentralisation and possibly the introduction of a market economy.

For all his political skills, Gorbachev discovered that the introduction of major reforms and the raising of expectations, whilst maintaining political and social stability, is an extremely delicate operation, fraught with hazards, not least for the leadership. It is in this light that the success or failure of *Perestroika* has to be measured.

A Gorbachev On Reform

Every readjustment of the economic mechanism begins with a readjustment of thinking, with a rejection of old stereotypes of thought and actions, with a clear understanding of the new tasks. This refers primarily to the activity of our economic personnel, to the functionaries of the central links of administration. Most of them have a clear idea of the Party's initiatives and seek and find the best ways of carrying them out. . . . It is hard, however, to understand those who take a 'wait and see' policy, or those who do not actually do anything or change anything. There will be no reconciliation with the stance taken by functionaries of that kind. We will simply have to part ways with them. All the more so do we have to part ways with those who hope that everything will settle down and return to the old lines. That will not happen, comrades!

Report by Gorbachev to the Twenty-Seventh Congress of the Communist Party, 25 February 1986

B Agricultural Reform

It is an open secret that the social problems are very complicated in the countryside, and the peasant also has numerous other woes. In the past six years the shifts in the development of agricultural production and its economics have become more conspicuous and steady advance has been made in livestock farming. However, no substantial improvement has taken place in supplies. Shortages breed covert and overt black-marketeering; social justice is all too often flagrantly violated; hence popular discontent.

V. Nikonov, a member of the Politburo: *What's Good For The Farmer Is Good For The Country* (Moscow 1989)

C Continuing Problems

The birth rate has gone up, while the death rate has dropped. This is related to no small extent to the war we have declared on hard drinking and alcoholism. These are the tangible fruits of *perestroika*.' But, comrades, we have got to be self-critical; we must see clearly that despite all the positive effects, the state of affairs in the economy is changing too slowly. Some advances are on hand. But they cannot satisfy us. In substance, the increase we have achieved in food output has largely been used to cover the demand connected with the growth of the population. . . . And those who are holding up the process, who are creating hindrances, have got to be put out of the way.

Difficulties arose largely due to the tenacity of managerial stereotypes, to a striving to conserve familiar command methods of economic management, to the resistance of a part of the managerial *cadre*. Indeed, we are running into undisguised attempts at perverting the essence of the reform, at filling the new managerial forms with the old content. And what is most intolerable is that enterprises are being compelled by means of state orders to manufacture goods that are not in demand, compelled for the simple reason that they want to attain the notorious 'gross output' targets. . . . Enterprises that have been given the right to reward their more efficient workers and cut down on the incomes of those that are lazy, wasteful or idle, are using it much too timidly in fear of offending anyone. To put it plainly, the reform will not work, will not yield the results we expect, if it does not affect the personal interests of literally every person.

Address by Gorbachev to the Special Nineteenth Party Conference in Moscow, 28 June 1988

D Growth Rates, Real And Projected
ELEVENTH AND TWELFTH FIVE-YEAR PLANS

(Average percentage rate of change per annum)

	1981–5 Plan	1981–5 Actual	1986–90 Plan	1991–2000 Implied
National Income Utilised	3.4	3.2	3.5–4.1	5.1–5.3
Total Labour Productivity	2.5 est	3.7–4.2	3.7–4.2	6.5–7.6
Gross Industrial Output	4.7	3.7	3.9–4.4	4.9–5.2
Industrial Labour Productivity	3.6	3.2	4.2–4.6	
Gross Agricultural Output	2.5	1.1	2.7–3.0	
Total Investment	2.0	3.4	3.4–3.9	
Per Capita Real Income	3.1	2.3	2.5–2.8	3.4–4.6
State And Co-Operative Retail Sales	4.2	3.0	3.4–4.0	4.1–4.3

Statistics Derived From *Pravda*, 1985 and 1986

E The Limits Of Perestroika?
Our Party is a ruling party. And, although increasing the sovereignty of the Soviets, the Party is not going to renounce its leading role. . . . Notions that the economy in our socialist society can develop exclusively on the basis of market laws . . . are unfounded. . . . The market is not a panacea for all ills. . . . Copying the western model of

a market based on private ownership is fundamentally unacceptable to a socialist system of economic management founded on social ownership.

Speech by Politburo Member Y. Ligachev at Gorki, 5 August 1988

F Desperate Remedies

The Soviet citizen of today no longer accepts what he meekly tolerated in the past . . . the USSR is rapidly becoming a second-rate power. Improvement of the Soviet economy depends largely on how it integrates in the system of the international divison of labour. And the main thing is to work for the convertibility of the rouble. . . . We are being directly opposed by the bureaucratic sector of the population. . . . The situation on the consumer market, far from becoming less strained, has in many cases grown more acute and become intolerable. . . . The consequences could have been less painful if the government had approached the economic reform comprehensively, and had managed to stand up to the pressure of various industries and the old managerial structures that sought to keep their position and maintain command of administration.

Speech by Gorbachev to the Twenty-Eighth Party Congress, July 1990

G Perestroika In Action

(i) January 1988: 'Manager with lengthy service willing to place himself at the head of any collective. This offer does not apply to self-financing enterprises!'

Some managers found it difficult to adapt to the new industrial initiatives permitted under *Perestroika*.

(ii) July 1987: 'Spreading the sea broadly.'
Perestroika included an attack on bureaucracy.

(iii) June 1988: '300 cups of tea; Sugar – separately!'
Limitations on the sale of alcohol led to a big increase in illegal distilling, with a consequent run on sugar.

(iv) January 1989: 'The class Soviet decrees.'
Under Gorbachev, reform threatened to reach even the classroom.

(v) 1988 poster: 'Every superfluous official holds up work.'

„ПЕРЕСТРОИЛИСЬ"

(vi) 1987 poster: 'We have "reformed" '.
    The shields read: 'red tape', 'bribe-taking', 'careerism',
'incompetence', 'bureaucratism', 'show', 'conformism'.
Perestroika also has a military meaning. Here the bureaucratic
opponents of *Perestroika* form for the attack.

Questions

1 Compare and contrast Sources A, B, C and F in their portrayal of the problems of implementing Perestroika. **(8 marks)**

2 How useful is Source D in assessing the real and projected performance of the Soviet economy? **(8 marks)**

3 How would you assess the reliability of Source D? **(4 marks)**

4 What does Source E suggest about the difficulty of implementing radical reform? **(4 marks)**

5 a) What do the posters and pictures in Source G suggest about the progress of Perestroika in the late 1980s? **(6 marks)**
  b) How do the sources convey their message? **(6 marks)**

6 'Perestroika faced almost insuperable problems from the start.' Using Sources A–G, and your own knowledge, assess the validity of this statement. **(10 marks)**

12 DISSIDENCE

Dissidence, in the sense of the expression of opinions hostile to the ideology of the established regime, had existed since the Revolution, even in the darkest days of Stalinist persecution. Only in the recent era of *Glasnost* has the issue become less emotive, since there is no longer one system of identifiable beliefs to challenge.

Since 1945 dissidence has taken different forms. Religious dissidence was strongest amongst groups such as the Baptist activists who opposed Soviet laws which prevented the religious instruction of children and effectively prevented religious gatherings or the spreading of the faith. However, even in the generally more compliant Orthodox Church, there were examples of dissidence during the time of Krushchev and Brezhnev.

Dissidence has also been concerned with human rights; until the Gorbachev era such concerns were never held to be legitimate, since the official view was that the Soviet regime existed to protect the rights of individuals, and therefore calls for individual freedoms were pernicious attempts to undermine society. Most Soviet citizens accepted this view to the extent of showing little sympathy with well-known intellectual dissidents, who ironically aroused more interest in the West where the conception of individual rights came from a different tradition. Nevertheless, several intellectuals became prominent dissidents in the 1970s. Sakharov was a leading light in the Committee For The Defence Of Human Rights, founded in 1970, and was to suffer internal exile. Other citizens suffered through interpreting too literally the USSR's adherence to the Helsinki Accords on Human Rights. Many less well-known citizens expressed dissidence through unofficial trade union activity or other simple acts of defiance.

Dissidence has also been connected with nationalism. From 1971 many Soviet Jews began to demand the right to emigrate. In the 1970s and 80s nationalist activity in the Baltic Republics, the Ukraine and Georgia became more widespread. Brezhnev stressed the peculiar character of the 'Soviet State', which in reality meant a policy of Russification which provoked great hostility. Gorbachev therefore inherited a dangerous situation. In the late 1980s there were serious territorial disputes between Armenia and Azerbaijan, demonstrations by Crimean Tatars forcibly resettled by Stalin, and demonstrations in the Ukraine, Kazakhstan and Georgia. Perhaps even more threatening was the apparent determination of the Baltic Republics to achieve independence. Gorbachev ruled out the use of force and accepted that a radical restructuring of the Soviet Union was inevitable, but the precise nature of the new Federation was unclear and, ironically, nationalist agitation throughout the USSR prompted a strong resurgence of Russian nationalism in the Soviet heartland.

By 1989 there was only one labour camp for political prisoners still operating within the USSR. Intellectual and religious dissidence was merging into the general debate about social, political and moral values associated with *Glasnost*. However, the problem of nationalist dissidence remained acute and appeared as a threat to the very survival of the existing Federal structure, quite apart from Gorbachev's personal position. Gorbachev himself appeared to change his stance, and force was used against Baltic Nationalists early in 1991.

A An Appeal By Sakharov

A law on press and information must be drafted, widely discussed and adopted, with the aim not only of ending irresponsible and irrational censorship, but also of encouraging self-study in our society, fearless discussion, and the search for truth. The law must provide for the material resources of freedom of thought.

All anticonstitutional laws and decrees violating human rights must be abrogated.

Political prisoners must be amnestied and some of the recent political trials must be reviewed (for example, the Daniel-Sinyavsky and Ginzburg-Galansko cases). The camp regime of political prisoners must be promptly relaxed.

The exposure of Stalin must be carried through to the end, to the complete truth, and not just to the carefully weighed half truth dictated by caste considerations. . . .

The economic reform must be deepened in every way and the area of experimentation expanded, with conclusions based on the results.

A. Sakharov: *Progress, Coexistence And Intellectual Freedom* (1974)

B Socialist Democracy

. . . Democratization cannot come about automatically and I have no illusions about the difficulty of the struggle. But all the same, it is wrong to exclude the possibility of an alliance between the best of the intelligentsia supported by the people and the most forward-looking individuals in the governing *apparat*. . . . The actual time period will be determined by many factors, but it should take not less than ten or fifteen years. . . . We must make an effort to accumulate information, educate people and win them over, step by step. . . .

Without being blind to the shortcomings and flaws in the very foundations of our social structure and ideology, we should fairly quickly, but also with the utmost caution, remove all the decayed elements at the base of the structure, replacing them with something much more durable. At the same time attempts must be made to improve conditions on all levels higher up. The whole process must take place gradually, step by step. Something new can only be fashioned out of what has come before in previous stages of social development. This painstaking and difficult task must, in my opinion, be the main objective of the democratic movement, which has arisen in the healthiest section of the Party and includes a constantly growing number of honest individuals.

It is in no way a question of destroying the values of the October Revolution. Rather we must restore and purify them; they must be reinforced and built upon.

R. Medvedev: *On Socialist Democracy* (1975)

C Ethnic Unrest

The Soviet mass media have been running a massive campaign of disinformation about the Baltics. Correct information is blocked. Half-truths and distortions are combined with direct lies. Instead of the outdated threat from 'world imperialism' which no longer frightens anyone, an image of a new enemy, this time an internal one, is being deliberately and remorselessly created. . . . The popular movements are accused of separatism, extremism, anti-socialism, anti-Sovietism, and being anti-Russian. . . .

We will not give in to provocative attempts to divert our struggle against Stalinism and the centralised command and administrative system into ethnic conflicts. We believe that Russian people will not allow themselves to be exploited as a tool for putting pressure on other peoples' freedom.

We should give a clear and open warning: the time has passed when armed force could solve things. Tanks are not only an immoral political argument, they are no longer all-powerful. More importantly, any such recourse to force would throw the Soviet Union back into the ranks of the most backward and totalitarian states. . . .

Having embarked on the road to democracy and national revival, we hope for understanding and support from everyone who has linked his fate to the homeland of his ancestors. . . .

Russians, are you about to give up those rights when it comes to Russia itself? No nation will agree to join a large state if that means losing its national identity and its rights to the land of its forefathers. . . .

Appeal of the Three Popular Fronts of Estonia, Latvia and Lithuania to the Peoples of the Soviet Union, 1990

D Popular Cynicism In The Gorbachev Era

Stalin, Krushchev, Brezhnev and Gorbachev are travelling together in a train. The train breaks down. The track ahead is damaged.

'Fix it!' orders Stalin.

The engineers repair the train and the track, but still the train does not move.

'Shoot everyone!' orders Stalin.

Everyone is shot but still the train does not budge.

Stalin dies.

'Rehabilitate everyone!' orders Krushchev.

They are rehabilitated, but still the train will not move.

Krushchev is removed.

'Close the curtains,' orders Brezhnev, 'And pretend we're moving!'

Still the train does not move.

Brezhnev dies.

Gorbachev gets out and orders everyone to shout loudly, 'There are no rails, there are no sleepers!'

At school every child is asked to bring three roubles for the poor in Nicaragua. One child brings nothing. Asked why, he replies, 'My father doesn't believe there are any poor in Nicaragua.'

Next week, all the children are asked to bring three roubles for the trade unions in Nicaragua. Again the child brings nothing. Asked why, he replies, 'My father doesn't believe there are any trade unions in Nicaragua.'

Next week, all children are asked to bring three roubles for the Communist Party in Nicaragua. The child brings nine roubles. Asked why he has brought so much, he replies, 'Father says, if there is Communism in Nicaragua, there must be poor people and trade unions.'

Gorbachev tells the Party Congress that he wants to change the seating.

'Let all those who want capitalism sit on the right, the rest on the left.'

After everyone else has taken their new places, one deputy is still hesitating. Gorbachev asks him what is the matter.

'I believe in socialism but I want to live under capitalism' the unhappy deputy replies.

'Come up on to the platform then' declares Gorbachev.

Soviet Jokes, current in 1990

Questions

1 Explain the references in Source A to the Daniel-Sinyavsky and Ginzburg-Galanskov cases. **(4 marks)**

2 Using your own knowledge, assess the importance of Sakharov to the Dissident movement in the USSR. **(6 marks)**

3 To what extent had Sakharov's wishes, as outlined in Source A, been fulfilled in the USSR by the time of his death in 1989? **(6 marks)**

4 Compare and contrast Sources A and B as examples of Soviet dissidence. **(7 marks)**

5 a) Explain the context in which Source C was issued. **(4 marks)**
  b) How does Source C attempt to convey its message? **(4 marks)**
  c) Why, and with what consequences, did ethnic unrest become so important in the USSR in the Gorbachev era? **(7 marks)**

6 What do the jokes in Source D tell us about popular perceptions of Gorbachev and his policies? **(6 marks)**

13 SOCIAL PROBLEMS

Like any complex society, the USSR has long experienced social problems of many sorts. Some were recognised by previous regimes and efforts were made to deal with them; some were ignored, or not officially recognised as existing. Some problems appeared to worsen in the Gorbachev era, although to some extent *Glasnost* led to a more honest and thorough consideration of issues which had always existed to a greater or lesser degree.

Life for the masses has always been hard. Although living standards in the USSR improved considerably in the late 1950s and early 1960s, they were low by Western European standards. Conditions were particularly hard in rural areas and in the poorer Republics. In the 1970s real wages rose steadily and social services were improved, at least in urban areas. However, disturbing problems remained: one was housing, as the Soviet building industry had never been able to meet the demands of its expanding urban population. Overcrowding and inadequate facilities spawned a host of associated social problems, such as a high incidence of marital breakdown, alcoholism and a low birth rate.

In the 1980s other problems became evident: the first Workers' state obviously had not translated the early decrees on female emancipation into meaningful practice; the growth in consumption per head began to fall; the death rate increased, partly reflecting an increase in alcoholism; in 1989 rationing had to be reintroduced; the Black Market, and other illegal practices such as moonlighting, were on the increase, and indeed the economy depended upon them to work at all; and anti-social manifestations, such as teenage hooliganism, became more widespread. Dissatisfaction with the results of Gorbachev's reforms aggravated the situation. Reports of juvenile alienation and problems such as drug abuse, the existence of which was publicly acknowledged for the first time, suggested more difficulties for a beleaguered regime, even if they were not on the scale of such manifestations in the West.

Some of the social problems described were likely to occur in any complex society. However, they were probably exacerbated by the fact that in an era of reform and openness, peoples' sense of insecurity and different expectations made some aspects of life more difficult. The old days, when a Soviet citizen had, to a large extent, his or her life mapped out by a repressive but paternalistic regime, were gone; the new Soviet citizen had to take greater responsibility for his or her life – by no means an easy transition.

(A) January 1988: 'All households! District militia officers
approaching the neighbourhood!'

Limitations on the sale of alcohol stimulated an increase in
home-brewing. The authorities experienced great difficulty in
reducing the incidence of alcoholism.

(B) 1988 cartoon: 'Now children, let's begin the song: "I'll play upon the concertina." '

The attitude of young people caused increasing concern.

(C) 1988 cartoon: 'Here is a list of those who don't make home-distilled vodka in our region.'

(D) 'Don't you dare!'

(E) 'Why do grown-ups drink?'

(F) 1988 posters: The campaign against alcohol abuse, particularly involving children, was prominent under Gorbachev.

(G) 'Don't cripple him!'

(H) 1980s poster: 'The male way of life.'

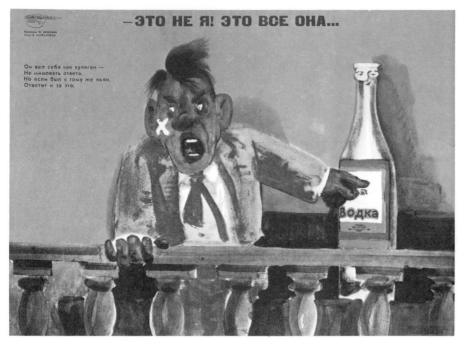

(I) 1980s poster: 'It's not me! It's all due to that . . .'

(J) 1980s poster: 'No admittance!' 'In the factory and works, mortal battle is declared against drunkenness.'

(K) 1980s poster: 'Look, we have completely removed the stain for you!'

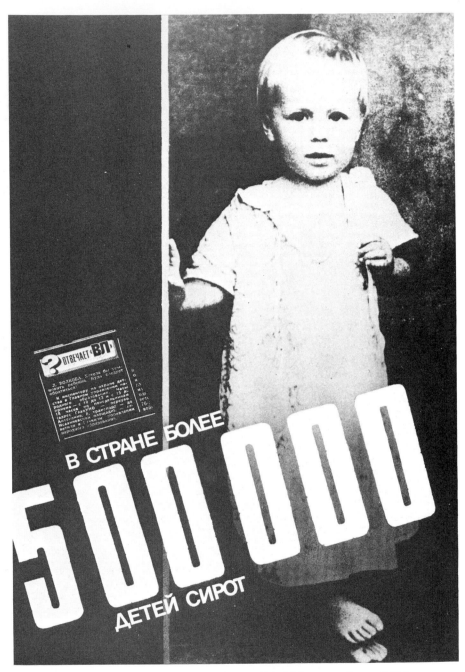

(L) 1988 poster: 'There are more than 500,000 parentless children in the USSR.'

A Children's Fund was set up in 1988.

(M) 1988 poster: 'Show concern!'
 The need for voluntary agencies was admitted for the first time
in Gorbachev's USSR.

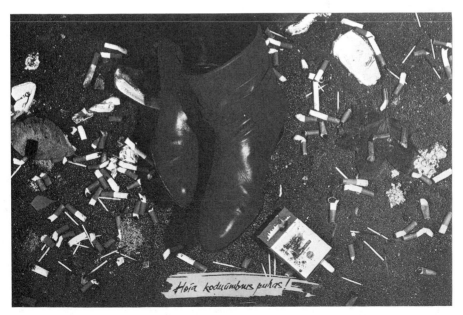

(N) 1988 poster: 'Keep Estonia tidy.'

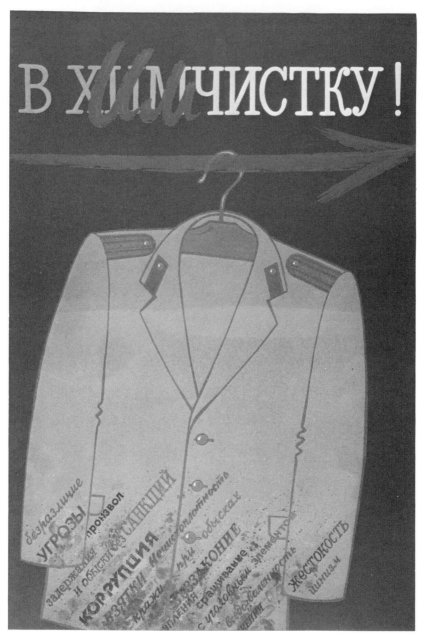

(O) 1988 poster: 'In need of a clean!'
   The policeman's uniform is stained by words such as
'arbitrariness', 'corruption', 'lawlessness' and 'cruelty'.

Questions

1 Identify the principal themes of these cartoons and posters. **(8 marks)**

2 What methods are used to convey these themes? **(8 marks)**

3 What are the uses and limitations of these sources in an investigation of Soviet society in the Gorbachev era? You should refer to examples from the sources in your answer. **(8 marks)**

14 HISTORIOGRAPHY IN THE USSR

Historiography in the USSR has undergone some shifts of emphasis since the Second World War. In Stalin's last years all interpretations of Soviet history were required to reflect the official line that all his policies had been correct, and any opposition was firmly denounced. In 1956 Krushchev's denunciation of Stalin allowed historians for the first time to investigate Stalinist policies through studying the evidence rather than adhering to an official line. However, in 1964 Krushchev's fall checked the process, probably due to the official fear that continued criticism of Stalin might lead to criticism of other individuals and the system itself. Historical misinterpretations were allowed to continue: for example, Brezhnev's cult of personality required a gross exaggeration of his supposed role in the War.

Glasnost permitted the discussion of previously prohibited topics such as Bukharin and Trotsky. Stalin's role in Soviet history was keenly discussed. By 1990 it was even possible to debate some aspects of Lenin's policies, previously regarded as too sacred to criticise. Gorbachev gave official approval to a reappraisal of Soviet history, despite dissent from within the Politburo, and at least some previously suppressed archive material was now made available for study. Soviet historians were more hesitant than Gorbachev, and opinions were divided.

History in schools suffered from these controversies, because in 1988 the old textbooks were withdrawn, and a considerable period elapsed whilst official replacements were produced.

The historical debate has been regarded as vital, since open debate about *Perestroika* was inevitably affected by perceptions of the recent Soviet past. Of particular interest was the debate as to how far Gorbachev's pragmatism was in keeping with Lenin's policies. All historians are influenced by the society in which they operate, and total objectivity is impossible. However, the role of the historian in a society such as the USSR, undergoing major and painful changes, has proved particularly crucial.

A Gorbachev On History

There should not be any blank pages in either our history or our literature. . . . In the seventieth year of our great revolution we must not put those who made the revolution in the shadow. We must value each of the seventy years of our Soviet history. The Party has told us about difficult matters; and we must not present them today through rose-coloured spectacles. Instead we must let the socialist law of truth have its way. . . . History has to be seen as it is. There was everything; there were mistakes, it was hard, but the country moved forward.

Address by Gorbachev to Editors and Media figures, February 1987

B The Extremes Of Historiography

At the present time two extremes have been clearly established in the evaluation of our historical past. A considerable section of the scholars are inert, lack strength and perhaps willingness to renounce deep-rooted stereotypes in the evaluation of historical phenomena, and continue to be attached to out-of-date conceptions. Another section of the historians has declared its viewpoint and, quite loudly enough, is demanding a re-examination and re-thinking of the whole heroic path of the Leninist party, to rewrite its whole history afresh. They are supported by several literary figures and publicists, speaking from nihilist positions. Both these extreme directions must be criticised. New thought must be elaborated, based on a profound, detailed and all-sided analysis of documentary sources, on a true Party approach to the evolution of the past and present.

Declaration by V. Grigorev, Head of the Department Of Science and Educational Establishments of the CP Central Committee, in *Pravda*, 15 July 1987

C The New History

It is impossible to agree with those who propose to forget history or utilise only a certain part of it. Now we all well understand that this point of view is unacceptable. We must know the history of our Fatherland profoundly, particularly after October. Knowledge of this history, knowledge of the cause of particular phenomena, causes which lie at the basis of the huge achievements of our state, and knowledge of the causes of the major errors, and the tragic events of our history – all this will allow us to draw lessons for the present day, when we want to renew society, to disclose more fully the potential of socialism and its values. Now that we really know our history better, we know the roots of many phenomena which have disturbed us all recently and which were a direct cause of the decisions that the *perestroika* of society was necessary. . . . For us no smoothing-out of history is acceptable. It already exists. And it is only a matter of showing it correctly. It is a matter of our honesty, responsibility and a scientific approach.

Address by Gorbachev to Representatives of the Media and the Arts, 8 January 1988

D Truth And History

The Party has begun a sober examination of the post-October history of our country, not least because many of our present troubles have their origins in yesterday's departures from the political, economic and moral principles of socialism. Learning the truth about history is difficult work, it stings many people to the quick. And some people generally did not want an honest discussion of the past. We are learning to see achievements and failures in a correct light, to evaluate objectively the contribution of all Soviet generations to the birth of Soviet society. . . .

This work helps to clean the path to the future. The CPSU intends to continue it, keeping silent about nothing, not sweetening the truth, however bitter it may be.

Speech by Gorbachev's Aide Razumovsky, on the Anniversary of Lenin's Birth, *Pravda*, 23 April 1988

Questions

1 What do Sources A–D suggest:
   a) about the role of History in the USSR before the Gorbachev era?
   (5 marks)
   b) about why history in the Gorbachev era was a matter of controversy?
   (5 marks)
   c) about why history has been an important part of the campaign for *Perestroika*? **(5 marks)**

2 Using your own knowledge, consider a major incident in Soviet history and explain how and why its historiographical interpretation has undergone change. **(8 marks)**

15 DEALING WITH EXAMINATION QUESTIONS

Specimen source question answer

(*See pages 28–35*)

1 Using your own knowledge, and Sources A, B and C, consider the extent to which the Soviet economy succeeded by 1982 in fulfilling the hopes expressed in the Sources. **(10 marks)**

The Sources present a generally optimistic view of the future. In Source A, Brezhnev describes an economic decline partly due to 'shortcomings in administration and planning' and other 'negative phenomena'. By implication he is probably blaming the Krushchev regime, overturned two years before this speech was made. However, Brezhnev is also implying that these problems can and will be overcome: the old and tested remedy of a new Five-year plan will produce benefits for industry and agriculture and an improved standard of living for the population generally.

In Source B, Kosygin describes a similar view of the future. Wages and consumer goods will increase in quantity; and the quality of life generally will improve.

Source C was written towards the end of the Brezhnev regime, in the early 1980s. It paints a similar picture: the new plan will improve productive capacity and the quality of consumer goods and services.

In essence, all three Sources say little about *current* achievements – in fact Source A highlights some of the problems – but dwell rather on planned improvements for the future.

It must be said that these Sources were all optimistic in the context of what was happening in the USSR at the time. By the 1960s the Stalinist model of a centralised and relatively inflexible command economy was already running into serious problems. Growth rates slowed during the Brezhnev era and initiative was stifled. The quality of consumer goods rose, but slowly, and quantities could not meet demand. By the 1980s improvements in social services could not disguise the fact that the death rate was actually increasing, shortages abounded and the Soviet economy was on the path to chaos. The hopes of Krushchev, that Communism would be a reality by 1980, or the optimistic statements in these Sources, would ave seemed hollow in 1982.

2 How democratic was the Constitution outlined in Source D?   (**6 marks**)

On paper the Brezhnev draft for a new Constitution looks democratic. The three classes of workers, peasants and intelligentsia are represented as being in unison, with everybody's interests represented in this State. The political rights and liberties of Soviet citizens are confirmed and indeed furthered. However, similar guarantees existed under the Stalin Constitution (1936), and in practice they had meant little. No clear indication is given of what a 'developed Socialist society' means in practice. The Government also retains an escape clause: people's rights are guaranteed only in so far as they do not work 'to the detriment of the Soviet people's interests' and that they relate to the 'purpose of strengthening the socialist system.' The State alone can determine these parameters, and therefore the proposed Constitution was hardly a guarantee of democracy in the Western liberal sense of the word.

3 Using your own knowledge of the period, explain the extent to which the claims made in Sources D and E were realised in practice.   (**7 marks**)

As implied in the answer to **2**, the claims made in the 1977 Constitution were not necessarily realised. The Brezhnev era was not one of free speech, or a free press, or the right to demonstrate. In fact a new clampdown on cultural activities began under Brezhnev, reversing the partial thaw of the Krushchev years. Daniel, Sinyavsky and other writers were tried, imprisoned or exiled. Human rights activists monitoring the Helsinki Agreements were persecuted. Many Soviet Jews were denied the opportunity to emigrate. Religious minorities were subject to sporadic persecution. Demands for individual liberty were not accepted as valid by the regime, since such demands were considered prejudicial to the interests of society as a whole.

Similarly, the claims made in Source E (written in 1977) were somewhat spurious. True, the working class was numerically the largest class in Soviet society; but it scarcely had a leading part in the running of State and social affairs. The State was managed by a stultifying bureaucracy. There were people of working class origin in the Party and bureaucracy, but the Party and bureaucracy were elite groups, rewarded for their loyalty with privileges denied the rest of the population.

Likewise, although the peasant may have 'grown up under socialism', by 1977 he had scarcely become a good socialist. The regime itself frequently complained about the tendency of farmers to devote more attention to their private plots than their collective farm responsibilities. Large differences remained between urban workers and peasants in terms of education, wages and social opportunities, as witnessed by the continuing desire of many peasants to leave the land.

With regard to the intelligentsia, it is true that many intellectuals put their services at the disposal of the State, but others were represented in the dissident movement, or at the very least were guarded in their attitude towards the regime.

4 Use Source F and your own knowledge to explain why agriculture had
been a problem for the Soviet Government since the Second World War.
(8 marks)

The reference to 'agro-industrial production' is probably to the reforms
implemented by Krushchev in the 1950s. These were an attempt to
rationalise and improve the system of agriculture. Source F points to one of
the problems – administrative confusion and a breakdown in
communications. Too many departments and a lack of clear direction
complicated matters.

Agriculture had always been a problem area for the USSR. It emerged
from the War with much land devastated. The regime gave priority to
industrial revival. Many peasants remained apathetic or sullenly compliant.
Krushchev's reforms had attempted to stimulate incentives and efficiency;
but, they had failed, together with his Virgin lands scheme, partly through
over-ambition and partly through obstructionism from hostile officials. Soviet
farms remained inefficient, and yields were low by Western standards.
Basically agriculture remained a problem because it suffered from the Stalinist
legacy: an attempt to supply an adequate amount of food to allow for rapid
industrialisation at the lowest cost in resources, to be achieved through a
centralised administrative system enforcing procurement quotas paid for at
a low price. Whilst *reasonably* efficient in extracting resources to feed the
towns, at least with basic necessities, it was a system which alienated the
producers and could not guarantee a continued ability to feed a growing
industrial population *and* provide a source of labour. Krushchev had recognised
this but had failed to reform the system thoroughly whilst Brezhnev scarcely
began to grasp the nettle, and hence the problems of Soviet agriculture
continued.

5a) What concerns of the regime are expressed in these posters?   **(6 marks)**

Several concerns of the regime are expressed in these sources. Sources (i)
and (iii) show a concern with agriculture: farmers are urged to devote 'loving
care and attention' to their farms and to produce more grain, reflecting the
regime's continuing concern to improve food output. Source (iv) is
propaganda aimed at the working class. Source (v) is propaganda for the
BAM (Baikal-Amur Railway), then under construction, a project to open up
Siberia for economic exploitation. Source (ii) shows a concern to uphold the
role of the Party as well as promoting industry.

5b) How do the posters attempt to convey their message?   **(6 marks)**

These posters are typical of Soviet propaganda throughout both the Stalinist
and post-Stalinist period. Workers and farmers are shown as upright, solid,
earnest toilers and citizens, dedicated to the cause of promoting socialism
and the interests of the Party. These stereotypes are standard in Soviet

propaganda. Idealised members of the working and peasant classes are shown larger than life – the implication is that no problem is insuperable if the ideologically motivated workers and peasants are devoted to the task of building socialism.

5c) How reliable are these posters as historical evidence? **(6 marks)**

The answer must be: 'reliable for what?' These posters are not particularly controversial in content since they are principally exhortations to work harder. No overtly false statements are made about the regime's problems or expectations. They may be taken as reliable in that they are typical representations of Soviet propaganda of this period and the concerns of the regime – which were to increase agricultural and industrial output. The issue of how effective such propaganda was and how that success can be evaluated is a different one.

Approaching Essay Questions

The key to writing successful history essays must always be in the last resort the ability to achieve relevance. In other words, you must answer the particular question set. Relevance is worth much more than length or a mass of detail. Accurate knowledge is also important, but only if it is employed to back up a particular argument, not for its own sake. Unanalytical narrative, or prepared answers to a topic which do not meet the requirements of the particular title set, are probably the commonest failings of examination answers. Conversely, the best answers are often concise, always relevant, analytical and show evidence of wide and thoughtful reading. Your command of the English language is not being tested as such, but you must be able to present your arguments effectively!

Plan your essays. Break the question down into its key components. What are the key phrases or words in the question? Give your essays a shape: an introduction which will introduce the main argument and possibly indicate how you hope to approach it; a logical main body, written in paragraphs (sometimes ignored by students!); and a conclusion which does not repeat the bulk of your essay but neatly draws together the threads. Other issues such as style and use of quotations are also important if you wish to write lucidly and well. As with most things in life, essay writing usually improves with practice!

In most of the history essays you encounter, you will be asked to evaluate a statement or quotation, or answer a direct question. There are usually different approaches you may adopt: therefore 'model' answers must be treated with caution. It is, for example, quite in order to approach a controversial issue by considering evidence which supports different sides of an argument. On the other hand, it is equally acceptable to argue a particular viewpoint, provided you can produce supporting evidence. Credit will usually be given if you show relevant knowledge of contemporary and/or more recent sources.

There are books available which deal in some depth with issues such as analytical reading, question analysis and essay-writing. Students may well find any of the following useful:

C. Brasher: *The Young Historian* (OUP 1970)
J. Cloake, V. Crinnon and S. Harrison: *The Modern History Manual* (Framework Press 1987)
J. Fines: *Studying To Succeed – History at 'A' Level and Beyond* (Longman 1986)

The following list of essay titles on The USSR 1945–90 includes suggestions (no more than suggestions!) on how to approach them; plus a specimen answer. Use them as part of your course or for examination practice.

Possible Essay Titles

1 How successfully had the USSR recovered from the effects of the Second World War by the time of Stalin's death in 1953?

This should be a straightforward assignment provided the student clearly analyses the state of the USSR in 1945. Attention is likely to be focused on the economy, and the degree to which the Stalinist system developed during the 1930s had been disrupted or adapted. However, attention might also be given to demographic (population) factors; psychological factors; social factors, such as working and living conditions; and political factors, such as the state of the Party. It ought to be possible to measure the degree of economic recovery by displaying an awareness of the projected and real achievements of the Fourth and Fifth Five-Year Plans. Other factors may be assessed; although the psychological impact is less easy to gauge. Politically, it should be enough to explain the degree to which the Stalinist system remained essentially intact and all-powerful right up to Stalin's death.

2 'The Soviet Union's prime need after the War was security.' To what extent was this concern the prime motivation of Stalin's post-war foreign policy, and to what extent did he succeed in achieving it?

This is clearly a two-part question, but there are several facets to it. It might be as well to assess what 'security' meant to the USSR: principally the creation of a buffer zone of satellite states in Eastern Europe and a weakened Germany. Candidates also need to consider Stalin's reactions at the great Conferences, notably Yalta and Potsdam, and assess his policies during the 1940s which saw the birth of the Cold War. It would also be interesting to consider the controversy as to how much Stalin initiated events, and to what extent he was responding, in incidents such as the Berlin Crisis.

The degree of success is another issue open to discussion. It might be argued that Stalin's behaviour, particularly over Germany, paved the way for the Western policy of Containment, signified by the creation of NATO, and in that sense the USSR could not feel secure. On the other hand, Stalinism seemed to be reasonably secure in Eastern Europe. There is plenty of scope for informed argument in this question.

3 'A good patriot but a bad Marxist.' Is this an accurate assessment of Stalin's career?

This question needs careful planning. Answers must display knowledge of Stalin's career from at least the mid 1920s, if not before. Was Stalin only interested in power, or was he concerned with the good of his country? Or were the two interdependent? There is scope for discussion here, although answers are likely to focus particularly on Stalin's role in the War, and possibly afterwards, as candidates assess the way in which Soviet interests were promoted.

To assess Stalin as a Marxist is difficult, if only because it is difficult to define Marxism exactly. Marx said different things at different times. Therefore candidates should analyse Stalinism in terms of its political and economic structures, and compare them with a 'Marxist' model. However, Marx was more concerned with analysing his society than predicting post-revolutionary society in detail, and therefore it would be dangerous to dismiss any post-revolutionary Soviet leader as a 'bad Marxist' with confidence.

4 To what extent did Stalinism outlive Stalin in the USSR?

This should be a straightforward assignment providing students can identify precisely what 'Stalinism' was: a highly centralised command economy; a dictatorship resting both on personal and one-party control, backed up by terror and measures of persuasion; a system of cultural and social controls; an essentially conservative, bureaucratic ethos. Students may then consider post-Stalinist Russia: modifications under Krushchev and Brezhnev and more radical changes under Gorbachev. It should be possible to assess the degree of change or continuity of these various factors, although there are areas of controversy: for example, did Krushchev's de-Stalinisation *fundamentally* alter the system?

5 How successful was Krushchev in carrying out his domestic reforms?

Answers must show an awareness of the reforms: agricultural; industrial; and political (the Party). De-Stalinisation should also be considered in this context. Krushchev fell from power partly because some of his reforms failed and partly because of fears, particularly amongst rivals and Party bureaucrats, that he might succeed. Foreign policy was another issue. Whether any of his reforms outlived him is an issue to be considered; also why those that failed did so – to some extent Krushchev was badly served by his bureaucracy.

6 What were the motives behind Krushchev's policy of de-Stalinisation, and what were the consequences of this policy for the USSR?

Obviously this question requires a two-part answer. The first part invites an analysis of Krushchev's motives: a mixture of personal ambition; a desire to prepare for domestic reform and a shift in foreign policy; and a desire to pave the way towards a collective, less dictatorial leadership. Students must decide the precise balance. Reference will probably be made to the 1956 Speech. Answers should not dwell at length on the actual process of de-Stalinisation but should attempt to assess the consequences: political rehabilitations, checks on the powers of the security forces and some attempts at reform. The reactions in Eastern Europe should be discussed only in so far as they had an impact within the USSR. More difficult may be an assessment of the limits of de-Stalinisation: Krushchev was forced to abandon some of his original policies, but some domestic reforms continued. An assessment of the extent to which the USSR was still 'Stalinist' by the late 1950s or early 1960s could be expected in a high-level answer.

7 Why was Krushchev removed from power in 1964?

To answer this question it is necessary to offer a broad assessment of the Krushchev era in the USSR and to analyse the various aspects of Krushchev's policies which led to his removal: the opposition to his political innovations, particularly in the structure of the Communist Party; the failures of his agricultural reforms; the climbdown over Cuba; the unrest in the satellite states prompted by de-Stalinisation; and dislike of his highly individualistic style as leader. A knowledgeable answer might also demonstrate awareness of the political infighting which took place at the time of Krushchev's removal and the motives of some of his opponents such as Shelepin, the ex-head of the KGB.

8 'Domestically a period of conservatism and stagnation.' Is this a valid interpretation of the Brezhnev Administration?

This question concerns all aspects of the Brezhnev years, but answers are likely to focus on political and economic aspects. The 'conservative' aspect can be dealt with by a discussion of Brezhnev and his methods: he was essentially cautious, of the centre, and preferred to govern by consensus. The unpredictability of the Krushchev era was not to be repeated. The bureaucrats and privileged *apparatchiks* preserved the status quo.

Economically, some reforms were attempted in agriculture and industry, but never to an extent which could have seriously challenged the nature of the command economy. Attitudes towards cultural issues also reflected the resistance to change.

9 To what extent had the USSR become a Superpower by the time of Brezhnev's death in 1982?

The starting point for this essay could be the emergence of the USSR as a world power at the end of World War Two; or the situation at the time of Krushchev's fall in 1964. The main thrust of the answer will be military and foreign policy developments between 1964 and 1982. Military developments include the growth of a powerful navy and the achievement of strategic parity with the USA, although the strain on the Soviet economy could also be discussed. Foreign policy developments should include Detente, since the attainment of a new status made the USSR willing to negotiate with the Americans as an equal. Brezhnev and his colleagues also pursued a global strategy, involving the Soviets in Asia, Africa and South America, and crushing signs of independence in Eastern Europe; however, the Soviets usually gained influence where the West was weak, rather than through successful intervention on its own part. Economically the USSR could not compete on equal terms.

10 How successfully did the USSR compete with the USA for world influence during the Brezhnev years (1964–1982)?

This is a variation on the previous question. Students must establish the areas in which the two Powers did exert influence, and in which ways: political and economic. Particular Soviet successes should be explored: the prestige gained from signing the SALT Agreements and better relations with West Germany. However, the limitations should also be stressed: for example the failures to establish a rapprochement with China and to create a strong foothold in South America; waning influence in Syria and Egypt; competition from the Chinese in the Third World. The essential weakness of the USSR vis-a-vis the USA was that the Soviets simply could not afford to spend as much as the Americans on establishing or maintaining global influence, and the effort cost the Soviet economy dearly.

11 Why, and with what success, did the USSR pursue a policy of Detente during the Brezhnev era?

This is a two-part question probably best approached by first establishing a definition of Detente and outlining its principal stages, culminating in the SALT I Agreements of the early 1970s. An investigation of the likely Soviet motives will probably focus on factors such as Soviet concern with a possible Sino-American rapprochement; concern at advances in American military technology; a desire for closer economic and trade links with the West; and the ideological justification for the continuation of Peaceful Co-existence.

The degree of success was limited and short-term. Attempts to build upon the success of SALT I and the European Security Conference were impeded by controversies over human rights and above all the Soviet invasion of

Afghanistan. The election of Reagan and intensified Western fears of Soviet expansionism completed the process.

12 Why was Mikhail Gorbachev able to emerge as leader of the USSR in the mid 1980s?

This is a fairly specialised question requiring a detailed knowledge of the political manoeuvring which followed the death of Brezhnev in 1982. An understanding of the reasons for the promotion of Andropov and the stop-gap Chernenko is necessary. Some awareness of Gorbachev's background and his relationship with Andropov is also required. An acceptance of the need for reform helped to secure Gorbachev's elevation to the Secretaryship in 1985. A good answer will probably conclude with an analysis of the process by which Gorbachev began immediately to remove opponents and promote supporters. However, for this question, students should not stray into the area of fundamental economic and political reform upon which Gorbachev was to embark.

13 Why did Gorbachev introduce the policy of *Perestroika*, and how successful was it down to 1990?

See specimen answer on pages 99–102.

14 How successfully did the USSR maintain its Superpower status during the decade of the 1980s?

Answers might well begin with an analysis of the factors which already threatened the Soviet position at the beginning of the decade, such as economic strains and the isolation of the USSR caused by the Afghanistan adventure and the ending of Detente. The situation was scarcely improved during the Andropov-Chernenko interregnum. The efforts of Gorbachev to overhaul foreign and defence policy should be discussed. Military forces were modernised but then reduced in strength. The new dialogue in Soviet-American relations and arms agreements should be analysed, together with attempts to maintain or improve links with the Third World. Some reference to the internal problems of the Soviet Empire is very relevant. Finally, the difficult task of assessing the international status of the USSR at the end of the decade is called for: Gorbachev had deliberately allowed a relaxation of control over Eastern Europe and accepted that the USSR was not a Superpower in the old sense, yet he had acquired enormous prestige in the world and had helped to initiate a process which led to a reassessment of the state of international relations generally.

15 To what extent has the Nationalities issue been a problem for Soviet Governments since the Second World War?

Firstly the problem of the Nationalities must be established: the relationship

97

of the Russians to the rest of their Empire. Then the approaches of different Governments may be assessed: Stalin's simple 'solution' of suppressing or deporting whole Nationalities; Brezhnev's equally harsh repression of outbreaks of ethnic unrest and attempts to 'Sovietise' his Empire; and finally the massive problems faced by Gorbachev. The demonstrations in the Baltic States and many other areas of the USSR should be considered, and how this relates to long-standing ethnic unrest and the expectations aroused by the policies of *Glasnost* and *Perestroika*.

16 How significant was the policy of *Glasnost* for the USSR?

A definition of *Glasnost* and its origins should be followed by an analysis of its significance in different spheres of Soviet life: as a necessary corollary of *Perestroika*; as a vehicle for opening up debates about the past and the need for reform of all types; but also as a force allowing the expression of criticism and causing problems for a regime running into difficulties in several areas, most notably the relatively slow pace of political and economic reform. Its impact on the perceptions of the USSR abroad might also be discussed.

17 Examine the extent to which the USSR has undergone a cultural revolution since World War Two.

Like most 'cultural' questions, this should hold no fears provided candidates have studied a reasonable range of material. Interpretations of 'culture' are usually generous, and unless specifically excluded in the question, it is legitimate to consider education and religion as well as the arts themselves.

Answers are likely to trace the trends of various regimes: the rigorous cultural controls and campaign against 'cosmopolitanism' of the later Stalin years; the limited thaw under Krushchev; renewed controls and orthodoxy under Brezhnev; the genuine cultural revolution in the era of *Glasnost*. It is important not to over-generalise: candidates attempting such a question should be able to quote examples, whether mainstream or otherwise. It would also be legitimate to focus on specific areas such as youth culture, for example.

18 Why have human rights been a major issue in the USSR since the death of Stalin?

Answers are likely to begin with an analysis of the situation pertaining at Stalin's death, possibly with reference to the Constitution with its paper guarantees of human rights. The impact of Krushchev's de-Stalinisation is obviously relevant, as is the increase in dissident activity under Brezhnev. The international context should be considered, particularly with reference to the Helsinki agreements. The very notion of human rights in a socialist as opposed to Western Liberal context might be discussed. The growing demands for freedoms of all sorts under *Glasnost* should be considered, with possibly an overall summary of the years since the War.

19 To what extent has the USSR undergone a social revolution since the death of Brezhnev (1982)?

This is not an easy question, and a careful definition of 'social revolution' is called for. An analysis of Soviet society at the time of Brezhnev's death is an obvious starting point: class, status, social mobility and controls – all the usual indices which sociologists and historians use. The difference between changed expectations and *actual* changes requires exploration; and the origins of these developments. In the era of *Glasnost* and *Perestroika*, did consumerism, educational change etc. actually occur on a significant scale, or were they simply subjects for discussion?

20 'A mental revolution about the past.' To what extent have Soviet historians been able to reappraise their past under the Gorbachev Administration?

There is plenty of material here for those who have studied the historiography of the period. Since the mid 1980s Soviet historians have debated all aspects of the past, especially Stalinism. Old names have been rehabilitated; even Trotsky has been mentioned. This is one of the consequences of *Glasnost*, although some areas of the past, particularly those surrounding Lenin, have often been treated cautiously. Answers should include specific examples.

Specimen Essay Answer

Why did Gorbachev introduce the policy of *Perestroika*, and how successful was it down to 1990?

The first five years of Gorbachev's Secretaryship of the Communist Party witnessed the appearance on the international scene of two words: *Glasnost* and *Perestroika*. *Perestroika*, or 'reconstruction', became the foundation of Gorbachev's reform programme for the Soviet economy.

Gorbachev had a reputation as a reformer before his elevation in 1985. Nevertheless, the strength of his often-stated commitment to reform surprised many observers at home and abroad. Between 1985 and 1990 his efforts to achieve his goals were almost continuous, and yet, despite virtually staking his political survival on the success of his programme, by 1990 the long-term prospects were very much in doubt.

Why did the policy of *Perestroika* emerge? The need for fundamental reform of the economy had long been evident to thoughtful observers. The Stalinist model of political control had been partially dismantled in the years following Stalin's death, and a system of government had evolved which was less reliant on personal dictatorship. However, the Stalinist economic model survived well into the 1980s. It was a model characterised by a high degree of centralised planning and controls which discouraged innovation. Economic and bureaucratic structures were dominated by careerists and Party *apparatchiks* who benefited from the system, and who faithfully reflected the Stalinist ethos of conservatism. The limited Krushchev reforms had failed, partly due to non-cooperation by a disgruntled bureaucracy. The Brezhnev years were years of stagnation: the economy was over-centralised and inefficient.

Reform had already begun under Andropov. His platform combined economic reform, anti-corruption measures and an improved defence capability, to match that of the USA. His plans won the approval of the defence and heavy industry lobbies. Andropov also promoted reformers like Gorbachev into the Politburo.

Andropov's death in 1984 led to the elevation of Chernenko, a Brezhnevite of the old line, favouring stability. However, his appointment was only a stop-gap, and his death in 1985 paved the way for Gorbachev.

Gorbachev was young enough to avoid the label of 'Stalinist'. Instead he represented a new technocratic, reforming breed of Party man. His economic reforms in the Stavropol region had been neither particularly radical nor successful – they were mainly a reversion to the 1930s idea of establishing centralised tractor and combine harvester stations to service local farms – but he had survived, partly due to the patronage of powerful friends such as Andropov. Immediately after his appointment Gorbachev was able to promote colleagues of a similar background, such as Ryzhkov and Nikonov. By early 1986 Gorbachev had a reforming majority in the Politburo and the Secretariat, and he was able to begin a purge of inefficiency and corruption in the higher and middle reaches of the Party and Government machines.

Disappointing levels of industrial production, shortages of consumer goods, blockages in communications, complaints over quality – all were evident abuses to be resolved. However, Gorbachev had to tread a difficult line between not alienating still-powerful Conservative forces of opposition, and utilising the willingness for change evident in many lower levels of Soviet society. Gorbachev had the astuteness to enlist Lenin in the struggle. In his book, entitled *Perestroika*, Gorbachev declared: 'We must learn from Lenin. He had the rare ability to sense at the right time the need for radical changes, for a reassessment of values, for a revision of theoretical directives and political slogans.'

Gorbachev estimated that the USSR needed a growth rate of at least 4 per cent each year to ensure the future of socialism and the continued status of his country as a Superpower. Yet the growth rate in 1984–5 was probably as low as 1.5 per cent. Failure to resurrect the ailing economy would ultimately threaten the internal stability of the USSR and the authority of the Party. Gorbachev blamed the sluggish economic performance on 'breaches of the law, bureaucratism, parasitism, drunkenness, prodigality, waste and other negative phenomena.' The message was clear: 'Every readjustment of the economic mechanism begins with a readjustment of thinking, with a rejection of old stereotypes of thought and actions, with a clear understanding of new tasks.'

Low agricultural yields and the necessity to import grain made the restructuring of agriculture one priority. In November 1985 a less centralised system of agricultural planning and direction was created, the State Agro-Industrial Committee (GOSAGROPROM), coordinating the six existing committees. The following year a scheme was initiated giving limited autonomy to state and collective farms: the State would fix five-year contracts with farms for the delivery of foodstuffs at set prices. Once the contracts were fulfilled, farms could sell the surplus to whom they liked, or keep it for their workers or for future investment. A system of brigade contracts, tried by Gorbachev in Stavropol in the early 1970s, was introduced into several areas in order to stimulate production.

In industry, Gorbachev felt that the technological gap between East and West, exemplified by the low levels of computer technology and automation in the USSR, was one of the principal causes of economic backwardness. Therefore *Perestroika* must involve modernisation. In 1986 a State Committee for Computer Technology and Information Science was established to develop a computer training programme both in and out of schools.

Perestroika also meant a drive for increased discipline at work, campaigns against inefficiency, corruption, shoddy workmanship and services, a reduction in alcoholism and associated absenteeism. Economic experiments in Hungary and China were observed and discussed. Planning was streamlined: several large ministries were merged in 1985 and 1986, and some super-ministries, for example energy, were created.

Local initiative had been lacking. Therefore factory managers were now given far more autonomy. Once the targets were met, managers could sell surpluses to the State, other factories or the public. Proceeds could be reinvested or distributed to the workers in bonuses or improved services. Management could negotiate loans with state banks and introduce cost-accounting methods. Inefficient enterprises might even be closed. The workers were to be encouraged by the promises of more bonuses and higher differentials for skilled workers. The Plan for 1986–90 envisaged an increase in National Income and industrial output of about 4 per cent, an increase in agricultural output of about 3 per cent, and a rise in labour productivity of over 4 per cent.

How effective were these measures? In agriculture the effects of *Perestroika* by 1990 were limited. Complaints abounded from farmers that they were thwarted by uncooperative or hostile bureaucrats. Colleagues were sometimes jealous. Ironically, at a time when crop yields had improved, there were not enough labourers to bring in the harvest. Inadequate transport facilities continued to result in produce rotting before it reached its destined market.

In industry and commerce the effects of *Perestroika* were also limited. In 1986 a slump in world oil prices reduced Soviet export values by one third. 12 per cent of the national budget was spent on subsidising food production, but proposals to phase this out in favour of realistic retail prices met considerable resistance. In 1987 experiments which permitted private and cooperative ventures met mixed success: reluctant bureaucrats created difficulties over licensing. Many factory managers did not welcome new technology – it required the adaptation and flexibility to which they were not accustomed. Over one third of all industrial workers were still engaged in loading, unloading or repair work.

The results of *Perestroika* for individual citizens were mixed. The growing practice of linking wage funds of enterprises to sales revenue produced greater variations in wages. Women still tended to work in unskilled and semi-skilled jobs. However, more important to the average citizen was not the level of wages but the fact that shortages of goods in the shops and poor quality remained a serious problem, compounded by the fact that from 1989 rationing was reintroduced. Basic commodities, such as tea, coffee, sugar and cigarettes, were increasingly in short supply. Many Soviet citizens were convinced either that *Perestroika* had, literally, failed to deliver the goods, or that it had nothing to offer them anyway.

Reformers like Gorbachev were obviously coming to the same conclusion. Having for years asserted that *Perestroika* did not mean the end of Socialism and the introduction of a market economy, in September 1990 Gorbachev came out in favour of the radical Shatalin Plan. This Plan envisaged a switch to a market economy over a 500 day period, and included proposals such as opening a stock exchange and closing or privatising the largest state enterprises; whilst prices would rise to reach their own level and unemployment would drastically increase.

By 1990 it was clear to most people that on the success of *Perestroika* depended the survival of Gorbachev and the new era of *Glasnost* and reform. Either *Perestroika* must succeed in the near future, or the danger was a reaction from the Right, suspicious of what was seen as the restoration of capitalism; or a complete collapse of the economy, leading perhaps to anarchy or a military coup. By 1990 *Perestroika* had promised much but had failed thus far to deliver.

BIBLIOGRAPHY

This bibliography is not exhaustive. Extensive bibliographies may be found in many books and monographs on Soviet History. Nevertheless the books listed below are a useful resource for the period 1945–90, they should be readily accessible to students and teachers, and they are all available in paperback.

R. Edmonds: *Soviet Foreign Policy: The Brezhnev Years* (OUP 1983). A detailed account and analysis of Soviet foreign policy during the 1960s and 1970s.

G. Gill: *Stalinism* (Macmillan 1990). A short, analytical account of Stalin's career and its importance. There is a useful section on the nature of Stalinism and its legacy for the USSR.

B. Kerblay: *Modern Soviet Society* (Methuen 1983). A detailed sociological analysis of the USSR in the Brezhnev era. There are detailed analyses of several aspects of Soviet life, based on extensive research of Soviet sources.

M. Lynch: *Stalin And Krushchev: The USSR 1924–64* (Hodder and Stoughton 1990). This book has been written specifically for A-Level and Higher Grade students, and combines useful narrative and analysis, along with exercises.

ed. **M. McCauley:** *Krushchev And Krushchevism* (Macmillan 1987). A selection of essays by several authors on all aspects of Krushchev's domestic and foreign policies.

ed. **M. McCauley:** *The Soviet Union Under Gorbachev* (Abacus 1987). A detailed selection of essays by several authors, dealing with different aspects of the first three years of the Gorbachev era – the leadership, politics, the economy, foreign and defence policies, and relations with the Nationalities.

P. Mooney: *The Soviet Superpower: The Soviet Union 1945–80* (Heinemann 1982). A detailed textbook covering both the domestic and foreign policies of the late Stalin, Krushchev and Brezhnev eras.

J. Steele: *The Limits Of Soviet Power: The Kremlin's Foreign Policy – Brezhnev To Chernenko* (Penguin Books 1985). A revisionist analysis of Soviet policy.

M. Walker: *The Waking Giant: The Soviet Union Under Gorbachev* (Abacus 1987). By the former *Guardian* correspondent in Moscow. There are useful chapters on the rise of Gorbachev, his policies, the realities of *Glasnost* and *Perestroika*, and social developments in the USSR.

M. Walker: *Martin Walker's Russia* (Abacus 1989). A collection of *Guardian* articles, with little on the politics, but a readable and varied collection of articles giving an insight into the everyday lives of Soviet citizens in the 1980s.

INDEX